HOW TO HANDLE

STAFF MISCONDUCT

HOW TO HANDLE
STAFF
MISCONDUCT

A Step-by-Step Guide

C. Edward Lawrence
Myra K. Vachon

CORWIN PRESS, INC.
A Sage Publications Company
Thousand Oaks, California

For information address:

 Corwin Press, Inc.
2455 Teller Road
Thousand Oaks, California 91320

SAGE Publications Ltd.
6 Bonhill Street
London EC2A 4PU
United Kingdom

SAGE Publications India Pvt. Ltd.
M-32 Market
Greater Kailash I
New Delhi 110 048 India

Printed in the United States of America

Library of Congress Cataloging-in-Publication Data

Lawrence, C. Edward.
    How to handle staff misconduct: A step-by-step guide /authors,
  C. Edward Lawrence, Myra K. Vachon.
      p. cm.
    Includes bibliographical references and index.
    ISBN 0-8039-6185-5 (pb: alk. paper)
    1. School personnel management—United States. 2. Labor
discipline—United States. 3. Documentation—United States.
4. School employees—Dismissal of—United States. I. Vachon, Myra
K. II. Title
LB2831.58.L38 1995
371.2'01'0973—dc20

This book is printed on acid-free paper.

95 96 97 98 99 10 9 8 7 6 5 4 3 2 1

Corwin Production Editor: Yvonne Könneker

Contents

List of Sample Documents

A Cautionary Note

Preface

As a school administrator, you are often faced with the need to take action for inappropriate conduct of staff members. Because of the importance of following procedural and substantive due process, you must thoroughly investigate the situation, organize sufficient documentation, follow contractual provisions, and render a decision with regard to appropriate disciplinary action. If just cause cannot be substantiated or contractual time lines are not followed, an arbitrator may not uphold the disciplinary action taken by the school administrator and the school district.

This guide provides a general overview of procedures that you may follow in staff misconduct situations. Nevertheless, it is impossible to develop a "misconduct cookbook" to cover all cases of allegations involving staff members in all bargaining units. Even though commonalities may be present in certain misconduct cases, the combination of circumstances is usually different in each situation. Thus we are not implying that the examples used in *How to Handle Staff Misconduct* are the only methods or procedures.

This guide is intended to illustrate reasonable actions that you, as the school administrator, should take when a staff member fails to follow district policies, school procedures, and/or your directives. Numerous tips are listed to help you avoid the pitfalls you may encounter as you go through the misconduct process. Also included are sample letters and forms that you can adapt and modify to fit specific situations and to meet misconduct guidelines established by your own school district. Therefore, before using this or any other guide, you should thoroughly review your own district's misconduct procedures for dealing with staff.

The following categories of staff misconduct are also presented in this manual:

- Serious misconduct that requires immediate removal from school
- Sexually related misconduct
- Controlled substances
- Theft and fraud
- Misconduct outside the school setting
- Abusive, insulting, and/or profane language
- Corporal punishment
- Insubordination
- Neglect of duty
- Tardiness

In addition, you will also find information to help you prepare for and present the misconduct case to an impartial hearing officer, who may be a district administrator, the board of education, a mediation service, or an arbitrator.

This guide evolved through the experiences of the authors and through input from colleagues and school administrators during university classes. At these classes, it became evident that school administrators wanted and needed guidance so as to take action when allegations of misconduct are made against staff members.

We thank these colleagues and school administrators for their input and feedback, which was vital to the completion of this guide. Finally, we acknowledge the support, encouragement, and editorial assistance provided by the staff at Corwin Press, especially Gracia A. Alkema.

How to Use This Guide

First, thoroughly read the Introduction and Part I, which includes Chapter 1, "General Misconduct Procedures"; Chapter 2, "Serious Misconduct Requiring Immediate Suspension"; Chapter 3, "Presenting the Misconduct Case at a Hearing"; and Chapter 4, "Misconduct Charge Statements." Then, scan Part II to become familiar with the remaining chapters, which focus on procedures for dealing with the different categories of misconduct.

When an incident occurs that is potential misconduct, you will have a basic understanding of the misconduct process and can then go to the chapter in Part II that deals specifically with the type of incident involved. Each of these chapters contains references to other chapters, sample documents, and resources that you can use as you continue through the misconduct process.

In cases where the employee must be removed immediately from the school setting because of serious misconduct, the proceedings will probably move beyond the school level before a resolution is reached. For assistance with this situation, you are directed to Chapter 2, "Serious Misconduct Requiring Immediate Suspension," and the appropriate sample documents.

This guide does not replace advisement and consultation available to you within your school district. It does, however, present basic guidance and cautions to ensure due process during misconduct proceedings. If you receive advice from your supervisor, attorney for the school district, or director of personnel that is contrary to information in this publication, you should follow their advice because of their historical knowledge of misconduct cases in your school district. Although you may want to propose a different approach from the one that your advisers recommend, you should follow their advice.

About the Authors

C. Edward Lawrence is Assistant Superintendent of School Administrative Support and Accountability for the Milwaukee School District in Milwaukee, Wisconsin. He has had an extensive career in education in the Milwaukee School District. He has served as a teacher, counselor, team leader, assistant principal at the elementary, middle, and high school levels, elementary and middle school principal, director of alternative programs, and community superintendent. He has been a hearing officer for immediate suspension, second-step misconduct cases, and unsatisfactory teacher evaluations. Also, he has conducted workshops for school administrators on how to prepare and win unsatisfactory teacher evaluation and misconduct cases. He holds a Ph.D. in urban education from the University of Wisconsin–Milwaukee, where he is an adjunct instructor in the Department of Administrative Leadership, teaching courses in instructional supervision and school personnel. His most recent publication is *The Marginal Teacher: A Step-by-Step Guide to Fair Procedures for Identification and Dismissal* (1993).

Myra K. Vachon is Administrative Specialist for the Milwaukee School District in Milwaukee, Wisconsin. During her career in the Milwaukee School District, she has served as a teacher, department chairwoman, curriculum and instruction supervisor, school administrator, and assistant to community superintendent. She has supervised preservice and in-service classroom teachers, served as a hearing officer for second-step misconduct cases, advised school administrators with regard to teacher supervision procedures and techniques, and conducted workshops for school administrators on how to prepare and win unsatisfactory teacher evaluations and misconduct cases. She holds a Ph.D. in urban education from the University of Wisconsin–Milwaukee, where she has taught courses in the Department of Administrative Leadership on supervising instructional staff. Also, she has served as adjunct instructor at Alverno College–Milwaukee in the Education Department teaching a science methods course for elementary school teachers. *The Marginal Teacher: A Step-by-Step Guide to Fair Procedures for Identification and Dismissal* (1993) is her most recent publication.

Introduction

To be an effective school administrator, you must know how to successfully handle staff misconduct. Therefore you must begin the school year informing all staff members about policies, rules, and procedures that are designed to ensure effective operation of the school. Also, to reduce the possibility of staff misconduct, you must develop a list of proactive tips to be included in the staff handbook. In addition, on the first day of the new school year, you should distribute a list of standards of acceptable conduct for all staff members. To meet the first step of just cause and ensure due process, you must provide all staff members with the foregoing information.

Unfortunately, staff misconduct hinders you from performing your primary responsibility of being the instructional leader for the school. In fact, the misconduct process may be very time consuming, emotionally draining, challenging, and frustrating. Therefore, if you have never been involved in a misconduct case, you may become discouraged because of the amount of time necessary to resolve the issue. It may take weeks, months, and even years to resolve one issue. Also, the entire process may cost the district hundreds of thousands of dollars for legal fees and back pay to a staff member who is reinstated after a lengthy suspension.

Frequently, administrators who lack experience handling misconduct cases recommend inappropriate dispositions (e.g., termination or other severe disciplinary action) against a staff member after the first incident for a less serious offense than an offense committed by another staff member. School administrators find themselves in a difficult situation when handling similar misconduct cases and they are inconsistent in their recommendations for resolution. When this occurs, the school administrator can be accused of racial and/or gender bias.

Parents, students, attorneys, board members, the superintendent, and other district personnel may question you about misconduct proceedings. Despite these outside pressures, you must maintain confidentiality about the alleged misconduct at all times.

Under the pressure of the misconduct process, your success and survival may depend on your conducting a fair and reasonable investigation to determine if sufficient evidence exists to prove that the misconduct occurred. Your decision to proceed with the misconduct case must be based on solid evidence that is without omissions or discrepancies in dates, times, and statements from the victim and the witnesses.

The evidence provided through firsthand knowledge of the alleged incident must be weighed carefully before a decision is rendered. If the preponderance of the evidence proves that the staff member engaged in misconduct that harmed students, other staff members, the school, and/or the school district, you must translate the allegation of misconduct into formal charges against the staff member that can be substantiated. In fact, you must have supportive documentation for each charge, and you must write the formal charges to allow yourself some flexibility.

This book is a quick reference guide for school administrators to use when handling allegations of misconduct that could lead to formal charges against a staff member. It covers a wide range of situations that can be applied to other disciplinary cases. The chapters provide information on general procedures for handling misconduct; misconduct requiring immediate suspension; presenting the misconduct case; sexually related misconduct; controlled substances; theft and misconduct outside the school setting; abusive, insulting, and/or profane language; corporal punishment; neglect of duty; and tardiness. Included in this guide are examples of standards of acceptable conduct for staff members, an allegation of misconduct report form, diagrams of the human body, the misconduct setting, major points of a letter of reprimand, progressive discipline log, and charts showing examples of misconduct, which can be used for comparison purposes to determine the disposition based on the school district's past practices.

Because contracts vary among staff members in different bargaining units, the misconduct procedures for staff members also vary. In this guide, the examples of letters are written for teacher misconduct; however, the same basic guidelines and content apply to activities of other classifications of staff members. Thus the specific contract involved should be reviewed in conjunction with this guide.

PART I

You should read Part I in its entirety to become familiar with the overall misconduct process.

1 General Misconduct Procedures

As a school administrator, remember that misconduct cases are confidential matters.

As a school administrator, you must have a firm understanding of the concepts of just cause, due process, and progressive discipline when handling staff misconduct. These concepts are the underpinnings for fair treatment of employees in all areas of the workplace. "Just cause" means that no staff member can be suspended without pay, reprimanded, or disciplined without good cause. "Due process" essentially means "fair play." "Progressive discipline" refers to a series of steps in which stricter disciplinary action is taken each time an employee commits an act of misconduct.

Chapter 1 discusses the concepts of just cause, due process, and progressive discipline. In addition, it presents an overview relative to the administrative investigation, the misconduct conference, charge statements, and any serious misconduct requiring immediate suspension.

Just Cause

You must meet the requirements of just cause to win misconduct cases. The "just cause" statement serves as the basis for the impartial hearing body to make decisions to determine whether or not the requirements were met. Thus you must be able to answer "yes" to the following questions:

3

1. Was the staff member notified relative to expected behavior and probable disciplinary consequences?   YES ＿＿ NO ＿＿
2. Did the staff member know the rule, conduct, and/or procedure, and was it (were they) reasonable?   YES ＿＿ NO ＿＿
3. Were efforts made to discover whether the rule or order of management was violated?   YES ＿＿ NO ＿＿
4. Was a fair and objective investigation conducted prior to disciplinary action?   YES ＿＿ NO ＿＿
5. Was there substantial evidence and documentation to prove the staff member guilty of the misconduct charge?   YES ＿＿ NO ＿＿
6. Was the disciplinary action relative to the seriousness and nature of the offense reasonable?   YES ＿＿ NO ＿＿
7. Was the treatment of this staff member consistent with the treatment of others disciplined for similar actions and under similar circumstances?   YES ＿＿ NO ＿＿

To answer "yes" to questions 1 and 2 of the just cause statement, you must ensure that staff members know expectations and consequences and that the expectations are reasonable. Therefore, at the beginning of the school year, you should provide a list of Standards of Acceptable Conduct for all staff members (see Sample Document 1.1) and explain that all staff members are expected to abide by the standards of acceptable conduct and the disciplinary consequences if they do not. Also, you must inform staff members that these standards are not limited to the examples provided on the list.

> Basic due process rights are embodied in the fourteenth amendment which guarantees that no state shall "deprive any person of life, liberty, or property without due process of law." Courts have established that a teacher's interest in public employment may entail significant "property" and "liberty" rights necessitating due process prior to employment termination. (McCarty & Cambron-McCabe, 1987, p. 380)

To answer "yes" to questions 3 and 4 of the just cause statement, it is critical that you conduct a fair and objective investigation and that you gather all facts and documentation necessary to prove the staff member's misconduct. Of course, you should use common sense when conducting the investigation. Also, you must conduct a reasonable investigation of the alleged incident in a timely manner and you must separate facts from fiction to make a determination if the misconduct occurred. If you delay conducting an investigation for several weeks to determine if the alleged incident took place, it will weaken the case and affect the ruling by a third party.

To answer "yes" to questions 5 and 6 of the just cause statement, substantial evidence must be provided to prove guilt. The disciplinary action must correspond with the seriousness and nature of the offense. Determining the appropriateness of the disciplinary action involves serious consideration of the following factors (Halloran, 1981, p. 3):

1. Circumstances surrounding the violation
2. Seriousness of the offense

3. Past record of the offender
4. Disciplinary action taken in similar situations

Even though each case is unique, you must look for commonalities to compare with other cases to determine the disposition. Therefore you should maintain a list of misconduct charges and dispositions. You must also avoid making arbitrary and capricious decisions when imposing discipline because it violates the staff member's right to substantive due process under the Fourteenth Amendment.

To answer "yes" to question 7 of the just cause statement, the disciplinary action must be consistent with the treatment of others disciplined for similar actions and under similar circumstances. Therefore you should review district misconduct files to determine previous disciplinary action taken in similar situations and maintain a list for future reference (see the sample documents in Chapter 4, "Misconduct Charge Statements").

Due Process

Due process provides the right of objective determination of disputed questions of fact based on established evidence. Simply stated, due process is the concept of "fair play." The staff member must be ensured of procedures encompassing the following elements (McCarty & Cambron-McCabe, 1987, p. 288):

- Notification of charges
- Opportunity for a hearing
- Adequate time to prepare a rebuttal to the charges
- Access to evidence and names of witnesses
- Hearing before an impartial tribunal
- Representation by legal counsel
- Opportunity to present evidence and witnesses
- Opportunity to cross-examine adverse witnesses
- Decision based on evidence and findings of the hearing
- Transcript or record of the hearing
- Opportunity to appeal an adverse decision

Many misconduct cases are lost in arbitration because of failure to follow procedural due process requirements.

Progressive Discipline

The purpose of the misconduct process is to correct staff behavior, not to impose punishment. "Progressive discipline" refers to a series of steps in which stricter disciplinary action is taken each time an employee commits an act of misconduct. At each step before termination, the goal should be to resolve the situation without the dismissal of the staff member. The steps in progressive discipline are as follows:

Step 1 Oral warning or oral reprimand
Step 2 Written warning or written reprimand
Step 3 Suspension without pay
Step 4 Termination

Oral Reprimand

The purpose of the oral reprimand conference is to hear the staff member's side of the issue and to ensure that he or she clearly understands rules, policies, and procedures as well as the consequences for not following these guidelines. An oral reprimand is given after the first offense to clarify the unacceptable conduct of the staff member and/or to explain where the staff members made a mistake without having to place a disciplinary letter in the employee's personnel file. To prevent small problems from becoming serious problems, no offense should be overlooked.

When issuing an oral reprimand to a staff member for an alleged misconduct or unacceptable standard of conduct, you must be aware of the proper sequence of steps. First, you should conduct an investigation to determine if the staff member committed the alleged offense. If there is sufficient evidence to indicate that misconduct has occurred, you must send a letter to the staff member to schedule an informal conference to discuss your concern (see Sample Document 1.2). It is important to hold the informal conference in the privacy of your office. Before the conference, review the major components of an oral reprimand (see Sample Document 1.3). At the beginning of the conference you must inform the staff member of the alleged offense committed and then give the staff member an opportunity to tell his or her side of the story. To gather further details about the alleged incident, you may occasionally ask questions. You can also let the staff member ramble without interruption. If, after hearing his or her explanation, you believe that misconduct occurred, verbally inform the staff member that the conduct is unacceptable and emphasize the standard of conduct that is expected. Finally, inform him or her that any future violations will result in further disciplinary action.

You must keep an open mind when you listen to the staff member. Try to have few or no preconceptions and refrain from judging the staff member before hearing his or her version of the incident. Also, it is important to keep your emotions under control and not to argue with the staff member. You may win the argument at the expense of losing the loyalty of an employee who simply made a mistake. After evaluating all sides of the case, give a constructive reprimand, without lecturing.

Even though an oral reprimand can be given in a pleasant manner, it must be firm, clear, and direct to avoid misunderstanding (Avins, 1972, p. 24). In this way, the staff member knows what will happen in the future and what he or she must do in the future to prevent another misconduct incident. Again, inform the staff member about the standards of acceptable conduct for all staff members. Try to end the meeting by giving some positive comments about the staff member. You should use the progressive discipline log to record the date, time, and oral reprimand message (see Sample Document 1.4). This will be helpful if a similar violation occurs.

Letter of Reprimand

A letter of reprimand serves as an official notice to the staff member summarizing the incident and testimony presented at the misconduct conference. In addition, the letter provides documentation in case the staff member is involved in any future allegations of misconduct. Listed below are key points to follow when issuing a letter of reprimand:

1. Use school stationery.
2. Date the letter.
3. Specify how the letter is being delivered or mailed.
4. Individualize the letter.
5. Specify the alleged misconduct.
6. Specify where and when the alleged misconduct took place (e.g., dates, times, places).
7. Clearly summarize what the witnesses observed.
8. Cite and quote the regulation broken.
9. Cite dates of previous oral reprimands and/or written warnings.
10. Provide suggestions on how to improve.
11. State that the letter is a written reprimand.
12. State that the staff member is being given another chance to improve.
13. State that failure to improve will result in further disciplinary action.
14. Refer to observations and follow-up conferences.
15. Invite the individual to state his or her own views in writing.
16. Give a copy of the letter to the staff member.
17. Place a copy of the letter in the personnel file.

(See Sample Document 1.5.)

Recommendation for Termination

When misconduct is serious or continues in spite of your efforts to correct the staff member's behavior, termination may be necessary. If the impartial hearing officer recommends the termination of a staff member, the officer should send a letter to the district administrator, who either concurs or does not concur with the recommendation. Based on the district administrator's response, the chief personnel director will issue a letter notifying the staff member of his or her termination. The master contract for various bargaining units contains a provision that enables the staff member to file a grievance and request a hearing before the full board or a committee of the board of education. The procedures and sample letters used when a misconduct proceeding is advanced to an impartial hearing officer can be found in Chapter 3.

The Investigation

When allegations of misconduct are made against a staff member, you must conduct a fair and timely investigation. Depending on the seriousness of the alleged incident, the staff member may be suspended immediately, with pay, pending completion of the administrative investigation (see Chapter 2). The same thorough investigation is necessary as just cause requires thorough investigation for all misconduct cases. The investigation should include collecting statements from witnesses and taking photographs and/or video recordings as well as obtaining reports from the police and other agencies as appropriate. In addition, you must avoid "shopping around" to get the answer that you want to hear about how to proceed or not proceed with the misconduct. There is no simple answer or solution to resolve a misconduct situation. Of course, you should discuss the misconduct with your immediate supervisor, the attorney for the school district, or the chief personnel director to get another person's perspective on the alleged misconduct. If you do have these discussions, be sure to inform each person about any other advice you received and from whom.

Victim/Witness Statement Form

Begin the investigation by using an Allegations of Staff Misconduct Report Form to gather facts about the incident from eyewitnesses (see Sample Document 1.6). Eyewitness testimony strengthens the case, *but* secondhand information or hearsay may not be credible. This victim/witness statement form must contain pertinent information such as report date, date of incident, name of staff member, time of the incident, location of the incident, and where the statement was taken. The form should also have space for the name of the student, address of the school, and space for the names of individuals who were present when the statement was given. In addition, the person making the statement should number and initial each page to verify the content. Space must be provided on the form for signatures, dates, and times.

When the victim or witness is completing the allegations of misconduct form, it is important that you as well as the assistant school administrator and/or the school secretary are present. If the victim or witness is a small child or an older child who has difficulty writing, the school secretary should transcribe the information to the form. If possible, you should first interview most of the witnesses to the alleged misconduct and do so in a different room than the victim. Then interview the victim. It is important that the witness and victim are not in the same area to collaborate on their statements. You may ask questions to clarify the incident, but do not coach the victim or witness. For example, ask when and where the incident occurred, what happened, and the names of witnesses. It is important that hearsay statements are not taken or used at the hearing. Also, the victim or witnesses must have firsthand knowledge of the incident. After gathering the statements, you should read the statement back to the witness or victim before it is signed. If there are corrections to the statement, the victim or witness must initial each change, including grammatical errors. Then the victim or witness must initial each page, and sign the certifying statement. It is critical that there is no conflicting testimony, in particular, dates and times. Finally, you must verify witness statements and cross-check documentation before presenting the information at the hearing.

Diagram of the Human Body

Depending on the allegation of misconduct, it may be necessary to use a diagram of the human body to describe the incident (see Sample Documents 1.7 and 1.8). The victim and/or witnesses are to show or point to the body part involved in the incident as well as circle the part(s) and initial on the diagram the part of the body involved. At the end of the form showing the human body diagram, space must be provided for the student's name, the name and address of the school, and names of the individuals certifying that the statement was made by the victim or witness.

Police Records

If the staff member was arrested, you should contact the police to get a copy of the police report and criminal complaint.

Photographs and Video Recordings

You may also consider using photographs or video recordings to gain a better understanding of the incident or to clarify points, taking as many photographs as necessary to gather the facts about the incident. If you use photographs to gather information about the incident, include a section on the investigative report that lists the brand and model of camera, date and time the photographs were taken, name of the photographer, date the film was developed, place where prints were made, and who had possession of the photographs or video recording before the evidence was presented at the hearing.

After completing the investigation, you must weigh the evidence to make sure that there are no gaping holes in the evidence presented. Also, to get another point of view on how to proceed with addressing the misconduct or to determine if there is enough evidence to proceed in addressing the misconduct, you may wish to review the evidence gathered with a third party. For example, you may wish to confer with the attorney for the school district or with your immediate supervisor. When presenting these facts to a third party, it is critical that you organize all facts in a logical sequence to avoid omitting key information about the incident.

After discussing the case with another administrator, you must decide whether or not to proceed with addressing the misconduct. If you choose to proceed, you must follow the procedures for misconduct outlined in the master contract. A letter must be sent to the staff member to schedule a meeting to present and hear testimony about the alleged misconduct (see Sample Document 1.9).

The Misconduct Conference

You should carefully plan for the conference that will be held to discuss the allegations of misconduct. At the conference you will conduct the proceedings, present documentation and evidence, listen to the staff member's response to the allegation, and render a disposition. In addition to documentation regarding the allegations of misconduct, have a copy of the master contract on your desk. Also, you should arrange to have an assistant principal or supervisor attend the conference to take notes and to verify what happened.

When holding the conference in your office, sit behind your desk and use the following seating arrangement as a guideline:

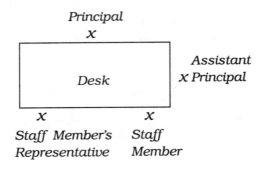

Principal
x

Desk

Assistant
x Principal

x
Staff Member's
Representative

x
Staff
Member

The following example demonstrates how to open the conference:

Greeting	"Good afternoon, Mr. VanderMurr."
Introductions if you do not know the staff member's representative	"I don't believe we've met. My name is Manuel Rodriguez. I am the principal of Duffy Middle School. Mr. Henry Felton is my assistant principal."
Acknowledgment of contractual provision and due process	"We are proceeding under Section III, paragraph (A), of the master contract to hear testimony regarding allegations of misconduct against Mr. Michael VanderMurr. The misconduct section of the master contract provides that substantive and procedural due process is followed."
Sequence of testimony	"I will present the findings of my investigation. I would like to proceed with my findings without interruptions. After finishing, you and your representative will have an opportunity to cross-examine me."
Clarification of procedure	"Are there any questions about the procedures for this conference? If not, let's proceed."

If the staff member brings an attorney and an association representative, ask the staff member to identify one official representative before proceeding with the conference. Any other individuals can only observe.

Even though you may present written documentation one item at a time, you should distribute a folder with all exhibits clearly labeled. This is a more organized way to present the information and will enhance the flow of the conference. Focus on the item being discussed by saying, "I am presenting Exhibit A." Present all evidence to substantiate the allegations of misconduct at the first hearing, because introduction of new evidence is usually not allowed at subsequent hearings. Also, your decision relative to continuing the misconduct proceeding must be based on evidence that you have collected and the evidence that the staff member and his or her representative present at the first conference. Always be careful about introducing new information after the first conference. If the case is taken to a higher level, however, documentation to support the staff member's testimony may be presented. If this happens and if the staff member opens up new areas for investigation, you should also take the opportunity for rebuttal and to provide exhibits to counter that testimony.

During cross-examination the defense will use various strategies to discredit your evidence and to intimidate you personally. They may accuse the victim and witnesses of collaborating on their stories. They will look for inconsistencies in victim and witness statements. They will try to create doubt in the believability of the evidence gathered during the investigation especially if there are inconsistencies and contradictions. Be prepared for the defense's use of highly combative techniques with you, the hearing officer, and the board, if the misconduct case proceeds to subsequent levels. The defense may accuse you of conducting an inferior investigation, point out spelling and grammatical errors in documentation, and say that you are a poor example of a school administrator. They may accuse you of favoritism toward some staff members. They may argue that you are biased based on gender, race, religion, or age or that you are in violation of First Amendment rights. No matter how frustrated or irritated you may become because of these accusations, do not exhibit facial signs of guilt, defensiveness, or aggravation during cross-examination.

Throughout the conference, be aware of body language that you project as well as the body language of the staff member. Even though gestures can be misunderstood and have different meanings, they can provide useful clues. In fact, you should watch the staff member for gestures that indicate that he or she is uncomfortable or feels guilty, such as the following:

- Increasing rate of eye blinking (usual frequency is 1/second or 60/minute)
- Not being able to look a person in the eye
- Taking glasses off and cleaning them repeatedly
- Rubbing back of neck (indicates person is annoyed)
- Sweating
- Scratching head
- Tapping fingers nervously
- Loosening collar or fidgeting with hair or a piece of clothing

To avoid disagreement and conflict over a possible resolution of the misconduct, you should close the conference by specifying the intent to review the situation and to adhere to the time line. The following example demonstrates how to close the conference:

Intent to review	"In closing this hearing today, I will review the documentation and the testimony that has been provided."
Next step	"Then I will contact you about my recommended resolution of the misconduct."
Reference to time line	"According to the master contract, I have seven (7) workdays to respond, but I will contact you before the end of next week."
Clarification of next step	"Do you have any questions?"
Farewell	"Good afternoon."

Charge Statements

After the school-level misconduct conference, you must weigh the preponderance of evidence to determine if the staff member's action was misconduct. If you decide to issue formal misconduct charges, you must be confident that they can be substantiated.

When reducing the allegations of misconduct to writing, you must substantiate each formal charge with supporting documentation. Write the formal charges to allow some flexibility for you to use the documentation to support the charge. You must carefully prepare the charge statement, which must be specific enough and written in such a way that the staff member will be able to respond (see the sample documents in Chapter 4, "Misconduct Charge Statements"). Also, keep in mind that one incident or combination of incidents may actually consist of multiple charges, but only charges identified in the notice can form the basis for termination (McCarty & Cambron-McCabe, 1987, p. 389). A critical element in such actions is to show justifiable cause for termination of employment. Failure to relate the charges to statutory grounds can invalidate the termination decision; that is, notice of discharge must clearly indicate conduct that warrants the legal charges (McCarty & Cambron-McCabe, 1987, p. 381). Moreover, you must follow up the charge by imposing discipline to ensure that the staff member adheres to the rule, policy, and/or guideline that was violated.

Serious Misconduct

Immediate suspension is appropriate for serious incidents such as theft, sexual contact with a student, gross insubordination, or fighting with another staff member in the presence of students. Chapter 2 describes the procedures that you should use to determine if the staff member must be immediately suspended from his or her school duties. The sample documents provided in Chapter 4 should be used by school administrators to prepare a ready reference with regard to previous disciplinary action taken by their school districts against staff members when allegations of misconduct have been substantiated. This ready reference will also serve as a guide to determine if immediate suspension is warranted.

Sample Document 1.1
Standards of Acceptable Conduct for Staff Members

All staff members are expected to conduct themselves as professionals to ensure the efficient, orderly operation of the school and to provide a safe learning environment for students. Listed below are some examples of standards of acceptable conduct for all staff members:

1. Report to work on time and refrain from leaving before the established time.
2. Perform assigned duties.
3. Attend staff meetings.
4. Follow reasonable administrative directives.
5. Refrain from engaging in sexual harassment of students and/or staff.
6. Refrain from any sexual conduct with students.
7. Refrain from using abusive, insulting, and/or profane language toward students.
8. Refrain from coming to work under the influence of alcohol/drugs or being in possession of a controlled substance.
9. Refrain from leaving students unsupervised.
10. Refrain from excessive use of the school telephone for personal calls.
11. Refrain from removing any school-owned equipment or supplies without written authorization of the principal.
12. Refrain from sleeping during duty time or in class while supervising children.
13. Refrain from using corporal punishment as defined by state statutes and board of education policy.
14. Refrain from using racial slurs toward student(s).
15. Maintain a professional working relationship with other staff members at all times.
16. Refrain from arguing or fighting with another staff member in the presence of students.
17. Refrain from distributing any flyers or other materials that are profane or vulgar or that have racial or gender slurs.
18. Refrain from conducting personal or other business during the workday.
19. Refrain from using influence over students or your position for profit.
20. Refrain from bringing guns or weapons to school.

If staff members fail to abide by these standards of acceptable conduct, including but not limited to the examples provided above, they may be subject to disciplinary action.

Sample Document 1.2
Letter Scheduling an Oral Reprimand Conference

ABC School District   Kennedy Elementary School
                                             1584 South Pineview Drive
                                             Crescent Ridge, CA 70799
                                                 (916) 444-8888

September 20, 199x

Mr. William Anthony
397 West Jackson Circle
Crescent Ridge, CA 70799

Dear Mr. Anthony:

I would like to meet with you as soon as possible to discuss an alleged incident involving you. Please see my secretary to schedule a conference this week.

Sincerely,

Lemmie Wade, Ph.D.
Principal

Sample Document 1.3
Major Components of an Oral Reprimand

Date	February 1, 199x
Time	4:00 p.m.–4:15 p.m.
Location	Principal's Office, Kennedy Elementary School
Individuals present	Dr. Lemmie Wade, Principal Mr. William Anthony, Teacher
Inform the staff member about the alleged offense	Mr. Anthony, students in your class have reported to me that on Wednesday, January 31, 199x, you told Noel, "Shut up, you stupid-ass little girl."
Ask the staff member for his or her side of the story *Listen with an open mind*	Tell me what happened. I guess I should have thought before I said anything. Noel kept asking Lawanda how to complete the paragraphs they were working on. She wouldn't read the directions for herself. It was a bad day . . . hmm . . . I was up late last night. Then my car wouldn't start this morning. It won't happen again.
Ask questions	You know, we have talked about the importance of building students' self-esteem and the emotional damage that can occur when students are called derogatory names.
Listen	Yes, it won't happen again.
Evaluate both sides and give constructive reprimand	Mr. Anthony, even though you said that you didn't mean to call Noel a "stupid-ass little girl," I must remind you that such language is unacceptable and should not be used by any staff member at Kennedy Elementary.
Let the staff member know what is expected and what will happen if a similar offense occurs in the future	You are to refrain from using any abusive or insulting language toward students. Any future incidents will result in further disciplinary action.

Sample Document 1.4
Progressive Discipline Log for Staff Misconduct

| Staff Member | Conference | | Misconduct Charge | Action Taken | | | |
	Date	Time		Oral Reprimand	Written Reprimand (1)	Written Reprimand (2)	Recommend Dismissal

Sample Document 1.5
Major Components of a Letter of Reprimand

School Letterhead

ABC School District

Kennedy Elementary School
1584 South Pineview Drive
Crescent Ridge, CA 70799
(916) 444-8888

Date

March 26, 199x

Mailing Designation

Certified Mail

Individualized Letter

Mr. William Anthony
397 West Jackson Circle
Crescent Ridge, CA 70799

Dear Mr. Anthony:

Identify conduct criticized and cite regulation broken

This letter of reprimand is being issued to you for continued violation of Board of Education Policy IICP, which clearly forbids staff members from using corporal punishment. Board of Education Policy IICP states the following: "Corporal punishment is not an acceptable form of discipline. Physical restraint may be applied only to prevent students from harming themselves, another student, or a staff member." In addition, you received the list of Standards of Acceptable Conduct for All Staff Members, which was distributed at the first staff meeting on August 28, 199x, and lists expectations for staff members. The standards are clear, direct, and unambiguous. In fact, Standard 13 states that staff members are expected to refrain from using corporal punishment as defined by state statutes and Board of Education policy.

Previous warnings and disciplinary actions

On Thursday, December 21, 199x, I met with you relative to an incident in which you held a student's arm behind her back and inflicted great pain. You were issued a verbal warning.

Suggestions for improvement

Three weeks later, I held a conference with you and Mr. Darren L. Miller, ABC Educators' Association, to discuss a second incident that occurred on Thursday, January 11, 199x. At that time, I reminded you about the Standards of Acceptable Conduct for All Staff Members and stated that you were responsible for improving your conduct and developing strategies for maintaining classroom discipline without using corporal punishment. Following the conference, I issued a letter of reprimand to you for pushing a student against the wall when he came into your room to give a message to his brother.

Specifics about the most recent incident

A third incident occurred on Monday, March 18, 199x. Students in your class provided written statements alleging that you pulled a female student's hair to force her out of her seat. Three parents complained to me about your use of force on the female student. Also, students in that class reported that you pulled the student's hair and pulled her out of her seat. Your continued use of corporal punishment cannot be condoned.

Intent of letter

This formal written reprimand is given to you to inform you that you will be suspended for five (5) school days for using corporal punishment. If you fail to correct your conduct, you will subject yourself to further disciplinary action up to and including termination from the ABC School District.

Allowance for staff member to respond

If you wish to respond to this letter in writing, I must receive your response within five (5) workdays. Your statement will be attached to a copy of this letter and placed in your district personnel file.

Closing

Sincerely,

Signature and name and title of the administrator

Lemmie Wade, Ph.D.
Principal

Copies

cc: Dr. Dawna M. Fitzgerald, Chief Personnel Director, ABC School District
Mr. Darren L. Miller, Representative, ABC Educators' Association

Sample Document 1.6
Allegations of Staff Misconduct Report Form

Report Date_____Date of Incident _____

Name of Accused Staff Member_____School_____

Time of Incident_____ Location of Incident_____

Location where statement was taken_____

I, ___(name)____, am a student/staff member at _____ School

located at _____ in _____, _____. I

am making this statement to _____, principal of _____ School,

in the presence of _____, assistant principal, and _____,

school secretary.

_____

_____

_____

_____

_____

_____

_____

_____

_____

_____

_____

_____

_____

_____

_____

_____

Initial of Victim_____Date_____   _____of_____pages
OR
Initial of Witness_____Date_____
Initial of Principal_____Date_____

_____

_____

_____

_____

_____

_____

_____

_____

_____

_____

_____

_____

_____

_____

_____

_____

_____

_____

_____

_____

_____

_____

_____

(continued)

Sample Document 1.6 (continued)

_____of_____pages

_____

_____

_____

_____

_____

_____

_____

_____

_____

_____

_____

_____

_____

_____

_____

_____

_____

The school principal read the above statement consisting of _____ pages to me. I initialed and dated each page of the report. I further certify that I initialed corrections in this statement. To the best of my firsthand knowledge of this incident, the above statement is the truth.

Signature of Victim_____Date_____Time_____
OR
Signature of Witness_____Date_____Time_____

Signature of Principal_____Date_____Time_____

Sample Document 1.7
Diagram of the Human Body (Front View)

The victim or witness should circle and initial the body part(s) involved in the incident.

a. hair
b. forehead
c. eye
d. nose
e. ear
f. cheek
g. mouth
h. throat
i. shoulder
j. breast
k. chest
l. upper arm
m. elbow
n. forearm
o. wrist
p. thumb
q. hand
r. finger
s. genitals
t. thigh
u. knee
v. leg
w. ankle
x. foot
y. toe

I, (name), am a student/staff member at _____ School located at _____, in _____. I certify that the above diagram shows the precise body part(s) that were affected in this incident. I circled and initialed the part of the body in the presence of _____, principal,_____, assistant principal, and _____, the school secretary, at _____ School. The circle, my initials, and my signature confirm that this is the truth to the best of my firsthand knowledge of this incident.

Signature of Victim _____ Date _____ Time _____
OR
Signature of Witness _____ Date _____ Time _____
Signature of Principal _____ Date _____ Time _____

Sample Document 1.8
Diagram of the Human Body (Back View)

The victim or witness should circle and initial the body part(s) involved in the incident.

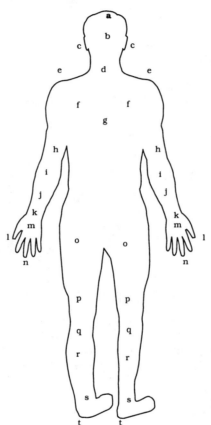

a.   hair
b.   head
c.   ear
d.   neck
e.   shoulder
f.   shoulder blade
g.   back
h.   upper arm
i.   elbow
j.   forearm
k.   wrist
l.   thumb
m.   hand
n.   finger
o.   buttocks
p.   thigh
q.   knee
r.   leg
s.   ankle
t.   heel

I, (name), am a student/staff member at _____ School located at _____, in _____. I certify that the above diagram shows the precise body part(s) that were affected in this incident. I circled and initialed the part of the body in the presence of _____, principal, _____, assistant principal, and_____, school secretary, at _____ School. The circle, my initials, and my signature confirm that this is the truth to the best of my firsthand knowledge of this incident.

Signature of Victim _____ Date _____ Time _____
OR
Signature of Witness _____ Date _____ Time _____
Signature of Principal _____ Date _____ Time _____

Sample Document 1.9
Letter Scheduling a Regular Misconduct Conference

ABC School District

Kennedy Elementary School
1584 South Pineview Drive
Crescent Ridge, CA 70799
(916) 444-8888

October 4, 199x

Mr. William Anthony
397 West Jackson Circle
Crescent Ridge, CA 70799

Dear Mr. Anthony:

This letter is to notify you that allegations have been made against you that may lead to misconduct proceedings.

A conference is scheduled on Friday, October 6, 199x, at 3:30 p.m. in my office to discuss these allegations. You are entitled to be represented at this conference by the ABC Educators' Association or legal counsel to ensure that due process is followed according to the master contract.

Sincerely,

Lemmie Wade, Ph.D.
Principal

cc: Mr. Darren L. Miller, Representative, ABC Educators' Association

2 Serious Misconduct Requiring Immediate Suspension

As a school administrator, you must make tough misconduct decisions.

When the allegation of misconduct is serious in nature and/or the staff member's presence would hinder the administrative investigation, it is necessary to immediately suspend him or her with pay during the investigation. Although the decision to immediately suspend the staff member must be based on sound evidence, it does not require that the administrative investigation be complete. The immediate suspension gives the school administrator time before the initial misconduct conference to conduct a thorough investigation without potential interference of the staff member involved in the alleged incident and to prevent complaints from parents and/or staff members who may be aware of the allegations. Depending on the size of the school district and contractual procedures, the letter releasing the staff member from his or her duties may be written by an administrator at the district level.

At this time, you must investigate the allegation and prepare to present testimony and documentation to the hearing officer with regard to the seriousness of the alleged misconduct and to justify the need to suspend the staff member. The hearing officer for the immediate suspension conference is usually an administrator at the district level.

Listed below are examples of misconduct that clearly indicate the need for an immediate suspension; however, other unacceptable conduct may warrant the same action depending on the situation:

- Gross insubordination
- Intoxication on the job

- Sexual relations with a student
- Pending criminal charges (e.g., drug-related crime, armed robbery, arson)
- Gross racial slurs
- Inciting a student walkout
- Excessive use of force against a student

When allegations of serious misconduct are made against a staff member that require immediate suspension from school, take the following steps:

❑ Conduct a preliminary investigation to collect information relative to the incident.
  - Use a standard form to collect statements from the student victim, witnesses, and other individuals, including parents, who have information about the alleged incident (e.g., students, staff, secretaries) (see Sample Documents 1.6, 1.7, and 1.8).
    — Remind the witness(es)/victim to be specific and include
      — when (date and time),
      — where (location or area),
      — who (first and last names of people involved or witnesses, if known),
      — what (events and actions).
    — Check the statements so the person providing the information can correct any inaccuracies such as in date or time.
    — Interview witnesses separately and follow up with pointed questions. Probe witnesses to ensure that all information is accurate and complete.
  - Take photographs of the classroom or area where the incident occurred, if appropriate.
  - Draw a diagram showing the location and any movement of persons involved.
  - Check the school and district administration files for previous progressive discipline information and/or misconduct letters.
  - Collect any supplemental documentation (e.g., board policy, staff handbook references, weekly bulletin references).
❑ Assess the information collected during the investigation to determine if the immediate suspension section of the master contract should be invoked.
❑ Obtain the immediate suspension letter, releasing the staff member from his or her responsibilities, from the appropriate district-level administrator and hand deliver it to the staff member (see Sample Document 2.1).
❑ Provide for coverage of the staff member's class.
❑ Escort the staff member from the building or make arrangements with security personnel or the police, if necessary.
❑ Seek counsel from a district-level administrator or attorney.
❑ Continue the investigation, and involve the police, if necessary.
  — Maintain notes of all conversations with representatives from agencies involved in the case.
❑ Prepare for the immediate suspension conference.
  - Review other cases that involve charges and circumstances similar to this misconduct charge.

- Organize the documentation.
  - Make a copy of each student's typed statement with the student's name omitted.
  - Make copies of all documentation for the staff member and the staff member's representative.
- If the evidence supports the allegations of misconduct, review resources available to determine the recommended disciplinary action against the staff member.
- Prepare an opening statement and personal notes to use as a guide during the conference.
  - Do not give the opening statement or personal notes to the staff member or to the staff member's representative.

❑ Attend the immediate suspension conference to present testimony and documentation to the hearing officer.

After the conference, the hearing officer will decide one of the following:

- To discontinue the matter because it does not warrant further action
- To continue the misconduct proceeding while the staff member reports to his or her assignment
- To continue the misconduct proceeding and continue the suspension without pay

Based on the decision, the hearing officer will send a letter to the staff member to inform him or her that no further action will be taken (see Sample Document 2.2) or to return to work during the misconduct proceedings (see Sample Document 2.3) or that the suspension will continue during the misconduct proceedings (see Sample Document 2.4).

❑ If the misconduct proceeds, send a letter scheduling a misconduct conference (see Sample Document 2.5). Then refer to the appropriate chapter in this guide for assistance with the steps to continue the process. In some cases, the staff member will request that the hearing be delayed because of a required court hearing or due to a school break. If this occurs, send a letter noting the request and informing the staff member that the misconduct proceedings will be reactivated after the court hearing or school break (see Sample Document 2.6).

Sample Document 2.1
*Letter Releasing the Staff Member From Duties Pending
an Administrative Investigation*

ABC School District

District Administrative Office
Department of Personnel, Suite 117
1062 West Scott Memorial Drive
Crescent Ridge, CA 70799
(916) 444-5555

October 23, 199x

Hand Delivered

Mr. Michael VanderMurr
482 West Valencia Court
Crescent Ridge, CA 70799

Dear Mr. VanderMurr:

An allegation against you has come to the attention of the school administration that requires your immediate suspension from all duties at Duffy Middle School effective on Monday, October 23, 199x, at 10:00 a.m. As specified under Section III, Paragraph (C), of the master contract, you are hereby suspended for five (5) workdays while an administrative investigation is being conducted.

A meeting will be held on October 27, 199x, at 3:00 p.m. in Suite 117 at the District Administration Office, 1062 West Scott Memorial Drive, to discuss the allegation of misconduct. At this conference, you are entitled to be represented by the ABC Educators' Association or legal counsel.

Sincerely,

Dawna M. Fitzgerald, Ph.D.
Chief Personnel Director

cc: Dr. Manuel Rodriguez, Principal, Duffy Middle School
     Ms. Lucy Erickson, Representative, ABC Educators' Association

Sample Document 2.2
Letter Notifying the Staff Member
That No Further Action Will Be Taken

ABC School District   District Administration Office
                                              Department of Personnel, Suite 117
                                                 1062 West Scott Memorial Drive
                                                      Crescent Ridge, CA 70799
                                                             (916) 444-5555

October 27, 199x

Certified Mail

Mr. Michael VanderMurr
482 West Valencia Court
Crescent Ridge, CA 70799

Dear Mr. VanderMurr:

In compliance with Section III, Paragraph (C), of the master contract, I held a conference with you and Ms. Lucy Erickson, ABC Educators' Association, in my office on Friday, October 27, 199x, relative to allegations of serious misconduct.

The testimony did not substantiate that probable cause exists to support the allegations of misconduct against you. Therefore no further action will be taken. You are to report to Duffy Middle School on Monday, October 30, 199x, at 8:00 a.m. to resume your duties.

Sincerely,

Dawna M. Fitzgerald, Ph.D.
Chief Personnel Director

cc: Dr. Manuel Rodriguez, Principal, Duffy Middle School
    Ms. Lucy Erickson, Representative, ABC Educators' Association

Sample Document 2.3
Letter Notifying the Staff Member
to Return to Work During the Misconduct Proceedings

ABC School District

District Administration Office
Department of Personnel, Suite 117
1062 West Scott Memorial Drive
Crescent Ridge, CA 70799
(916) 444-5555

October 27, 199x

Certified Mail

Mr. Michael VanderMurr
482 West Valencia Court
Crescent Ridge, CA 70799

Dear Mr. VanderMurr:

In compliance with Section III, Paragraph (C), of the master contract, I held a conference with you and Ms. Lucy Erickson, ABC Educators' Association, in my office on Friday, October 27, 199x, relative to allegations of serious misconduct.

The testimony substantiated that probable cause exists to support the allegations of misconduct against you. Therefore the case will move to the next level of the misconduct proceedings as specified in the master contract. Dr. Manuel Rodriguez, principal of Duffy Middle School, will notify you in writing relative to the date, time, and location of the conference. During the misconduct proceedings, you are to return to your assignment at Duffy Middle School and to resume your duties, effective Monday, October 30, 199x, at 8:00 a.m.

Sincerely,

Dawna M. Fitzgerald, Ph.D.
Chief Personnel Director

cc: Dr. Manuel Rodriguez, Principal, Duffy Middle School
    Ms. Lucy Erickson, Representative, ABC Educators' Association

Sample Document 2.4
Letter Notifying the Staff Member That Suspension
Will Continue During the Misconduct Proceedings

ABC School District   District Administration Office
                                 Department of Personnel, Suite 117
                                      1062 West Scott Memorial Drive
                                          Crescent Ridge, CA 70799
                                                  (916) 444-5555

October 27, 199x

Certified Mail

Mr. Michael VanderMurr
482 West Valencia Court
Crescent Ridge, CA 70799

Dear Mr. VanderMurr:

In compliance with Section III, Paragraph (C), of the master contract, I held a conference with you and Ms. Lucy Erickson, ABC Educators' Association, in my office on Friday, October 27, 199x, relative to allegations of serious misconduct.

The testimony substantiated that probable cause exists that you engaged in misconduct. Therefore the case will move to the next level of the misconduct proceedings as specified in the master contract. Dr. Manuel Rodriguez, principal of Duffy Middle School, will notify you in writing relative to the date, time, and location of the conference. During the misconduct proceedings, you will remain under suspension without pay.

Sincerely,

Dawna M. Fitzgerald, Ph.D.
Chief Personnel Director

cc: Dr. Manuel Rodriguez, Principal, Duffy Middle School
      Mr. Ling Yang, Compensation Director, ABC School District
      Ms. Lucy Erickson, Representative, ABC Educators' Association

Sample Document 2.5
*Letter Specifying the Charge(s) and Scheduling
a Conference With an Impartial Hearing Officer*

ABC School District

Duffy Middle School
543 Orange Drive
Crescent Ridge, CA 70799
(916) 444-3333

October 29, 199x

Certified Mail

Mr. Michael VanderMurr
482 West Valencia Court
Crescent Ridge, CA 70799

Dear Mr. VanderMurr:

As stipulated in Section III, Paragraph (A), of the master contract, a conference will be held on Thursday, November 2, 199x, at 2:30 p.m. in Suite 117 at the District Administration Office to consider allegations of misconduct against you. The charge is as follows:

- Inappropriate sexual conduct with a female student.

You are entitled to be represented at this conference by the ABC Educators' Association or legal counsel.

Sincerely,

Manuel Rodriguez, Ph.D.
Principal

cc: Dr. Dawna M. Fitzgerald, Chief Personnel Director
    Ms. Lucy Erickson, Representative, ABC Educators' Association

Sample Document 2.6
*Letter Notifying the Staff Member That the Hearing Has Been
Delayed Because of a Required Court Hearing or Due to a School Break*

ABC School District   Duffy Middle School
                                                    543 Orange Drive
                                              Crescent Ridge, CA 70799
                                                   (916) 444-3333

October 27, 199x

Certified Mail

Mr. Michael VanderMurr
482 West Valencia Court
Crescent Ridge, CA 70799

Dear Mr. VanderMurr:

A conference was scheduled on Thursday, November 2, 199x, at 2:30 p.m. in
Suite 117 at the District Administration Office to discuss allegations of misconduct
against you.

At the request of Ms. Lucy Erickson, representative for the ABC Educators'
Association, the misconduct proceedings will be postponed until after your court
hearing, which is scheduled for Wednesday, December 6, 199x. Even though the
misconduct hearing will be delayed, your suspension without pay will continue.
After the court hearing, you are to contact me personally to reactivate the
misconduct proceedings.

Sincerely,

Manuel Rodriguez, Ph.D.
Principal

cc: Dr. Dawna M. Fitzgerald, Chief Personnel Director, ABC School District
     Mr. Ling Yang, Compensation Director, ABC School District
     Ms. Lucy Erickson, Representative, ABC Educators' Association

3 Presenting the Misconduct Case at a Hearing

As a school adminstrator, never answer hypothetical questions during cross-examination at a misconduct hearing.

If a resolution cannot be reached in the misconduct process, it is necessary to involve an impartial hearing officer to hear testimony, review documentation, and render a decision. Master contracts of different bargaining units specify the procedures and time lines that must be followed when a misconduct case proceeds beyond the school level. Your role is to present the case to the impartial hearing officer. The role of the impartial hearing officer is to make the physical arrangements for the conference, conduct the conference by receiving testimony from both sides, reach a resolution, and carry the case forward if another step or steps are included in the school district's process. Additional levels that may be a part of the misconduct process include the third party hearing, school board hearing, grievance/arbitration hearing, and court hearing.

As part of the misconduct procedures, the staff member may appeal a decision or disposition to a third party. If the case moves to a higher level, the subsequent impartial hearing officer will examine the evidence in light of just cause, due process, and progressive discipline. In preparing for the hearing, you must develop notes to ensure that your presentation is well organized and that you include critical information. Your notes should include an opening statement citing the misconduct section of the master contract and expectations for all staff members, reference to due process, background information about the staff member's employment with the district and any previous disciplinary action taken because of misconduct, and concisely stated misconduct charges. In addition, it is important to separate the charges and provide pertinent information with regard to each charge. Therefore you should consider these elements in your investigation and deliberation *at the school level.* An example of notes for the third party hearing follows:

Opening statement

Section III of the master contract covers the misconduct procedures. We will follow those procedures during this conference to hear allegations of misconduct against Mr. William Anthony. I would like to present my documentation without interruption. Afterward, you may cross-examine me and present any documentation that you may have.

All staff members are important in operating a school where students can learn in a safe, orderly environment. All staff members are expected to abide by the rules of the Board of Education, the master contract, and the procedures and guidelines in the individual schools.

Due process reference

School procedures and guidelines at Kennedy Elementary School were made known to all staff members at the beginning of the school year. The same Standards of Acceptable Conduct have been applied to all staff members. No staff member has been singled out.

When a staff member's conduct is damaging to children, the staff, the school itself, or is in violation of school procedures and guidelines, misconduct procedures may be necessary to resolve the problem.

Background information

Mr. Anthony has been a teacher in the ABC School District since August 28, 199x, when he started teaching at Duffy Middle School. At the beginning of 199x-199x school year, Mr. Anthony transferred to Kennedy Elementary School, which is his present assignment. There are no misconduct letters in his district personnel file or in the file at Duffy Middle School. Since Mr. Anthony started teaching at Kennedy Elementary School, however, two misconduct charges were filed against him.

Mr. Anthony received an oral reprimand from me in my office on September 8, 199x, for failure to escort his students to the cafeteria for lunch.

On October 10, 199x, a misconduct conference was held in my office regarding Mr. Anthony's neglect of duty when he left his class unsupervised for 35 minutes. As a result, on October 17, 199x, Mr. Anthony received a letter of reprimand for failure to supervise his students.

Charge statements (state charges concisely)

Today, Mr. Anthony is being formally charged with three counts of misconduct. These charges are as follows:

1. Leaving students unsupervised in his classroom
2. Failure to maintain a harmonious working relationship with fellow staff members
3. Failure to complete and submit student grades as directed

Restatement of each charge

I will present each charge statement and supporting documentation for the individual charge.

Charge Statement 1

Leaving students unsupervised in the classroom

Questions to address

Date?

Time?

What happened (describe the incident)?

Supporting documentation

Supporting documentation and related exhibits for Charge Statement 1 include . . .

Charge Statement 2

Failure to maintain a harmonious working relationship with staff

Questions to address

Date?

Time?

What happened?

Supporting documentation

Supporting documentation and related exhibits for Charge Statement 2 include . . .

Charge Statement 3

Failure to complete and submit student grades as directed

Questions to address

Date?

Time?

What happened?

Supporting documentation   Supporting documentation and related exhibits
                                  for Charge Statement 3 include . . .

Summary statement   (Summarize all three charges briefly with a rec-
                                  ommendation to resolve the misconduct.)

The clincher   (This statement must emphasize that Mr.
                                  Anthony's misconduct is damaging to students,
                                  staff, and the school itself.)

— Do not use irrelevant facts.
— Do not use hearsay evidence.
— Do not include additional materials at the next-level meeting.

The board of education must decide whether the staff member is guilty beyond
a reasonable doubt. When presentations are made to the board of education,
they are usually conducted by the school district's attorney and the attorney
for the staff member. The questions directed to the school administrator usually
require a yes or no answer. At this hearing, the attorney for the staff member has
access to all evidence as well as to the names of witnesses, including students
who provided written statements. Also, for the first time in the process, the attorney for the staff member also has an opportunity to cross-examine all witnesses. The decision of the board of education is based on evidence and findings
of this hearing. A full transcript or record is made of the hearing and is available
for the staff member.

In addition, contracts between the board of education and the various
bargaining units traditionally contain a section outlining grievance procedures,
which give the staff member an opportunity to appeal an adverse decision. The
staff member may file a grievance alleging that the master contract was violated
and that due process was not followed. The staff member may have the grievance
appealed to the arbitration procedure of the master contract. The final decisions
of the arbitrator shall be final and binding on the board, the staff members'
association, and the staff member.

In some instances, a court hearing may be a collateral hearing, especially
if the misconduct involves a criminal act in or outside of the school setting. Because some misconduct cases take three or more years to settle, it is usually
difficult to remember facts. This places the defense at an advantage because
witnesses may not be able to recall facts, may have moved, or may have passed
away. Therefore you must maintain accurate notes and complete files.

*When the misconduct case cannot be resolved at the school level, take the
following steps:*

❑ Contact the impartial hearing officer to schedule a conference within the time
   line specified in the master contract.
❑ State the specific charge or charges in writing (see sample documents in Chapter
   4, "Misconduct Charge Statements").
❑ Send a letter to the staff member scheduling a conference with the impartial
   hearing officer (see Sample Document 3.1).

❑ Prepare for the misconduct conference.
  - Review all documentation presented at the first conference.
    — Present written statements and answer questions consistently in relation to date, time, and facts about the incident.
  - Make copies of all documentation for the hearing officer, the staff member, and the staff member's representative.
  - Review and update the opening statement and personal notes from the first conference, and use these as a guide during the conference.
    — Use essentially the same opening statement and personal notes as the ones used during the first conference.
    — Do not give the opening statement or personal notes to the staff member or to the staff member's representative.
  - Review "The Misconduct Conference" section in Chapter 1, "General Misconduct Procedures."
❑ Attend the misconduct conference and present testimony and documentation to the hearing officer.
    — Speak directly to the hearing officer and look him or her in the eye.
    — Be prepared to answer questions asked by the staff member's representative or attorney that are designed to discredit you as a credible witness. Your responses must be consistent relative to date, time, and facts about the incident.

The impartial hearing officer will follow the time line specified in the master contract and send a letter notifying the staff member about the recommendation to resolve the misconduct. The recommendation may be to dismiss the case (see Sample Document 3.2), to reduce the disciplinary action recommended by the school administrator (see Sample Document 3.3), to uphold the recommendation of the school administrator (see Sample Document 3.4), or to recommend termination (see Sample Document 3.5). A recommendation for termination is usually sent to the superintendent of schools for review. If the superintendent of schools concurs with the recommendation for termination, the hearing officer sends a letter to the staff member informing him or her that a hearing will be held with the board of education (see Sample Document 3.6). After the hearing in front of the board of education, the chief personnel director sends a letter to the staff member informing him or her that the board of education has reduced the disciplinary action (see Sample Document 3.7) or concurs with the recommendation for termination (see Sample Document 3.8).

Sample Document 3.1
Letter Specifying the Charge(s) and Scheduling
a Conference With an Impartial Hearing Officer

ABC School District   Kennedy Elementary School
                                                 1584 South Pineview Drive
                                                 Crescent Ridge, CA 70799
                                                     (916) 444-8888

May 17, 199x

Certified Mail

Mr. William Anthony
397 West Jackson Circle
Crescent Ridge, CA 70799

Dear Mr. Anthony:

As stipulated in the master contract, I held a conference with you and Mr. Darren L. Miller, ABC Educators' Association, in my office on Monday, May 13, 199x, to discuss allegations of misconduct against you. The formal disciplinary charge was as follows:

   • Inflicting corporal punishment on a student.

The proposed three-day suspension to resolve the issue was rejected. As a result, the next step in the misconduct process will be held on Thursday, May 23, 199x, at 1:15 p.m. in Suite 117 at the District Administration Office. Dr. Dawna M. Fitzgerald, Chief Personnel Director, will serve as the impartial hearing officer.

You are entitled to be represented by the ABC Educators' Association or legal counsel at this conference.

Sincerely,

Lemmie Wade, Ph.D.
Principal

cc: Dr. Dawna M. Fitzgerald, Chief Personnel Director, ABC School District
     Mr. Darren L. Miller, Representative, ABC Educators' Association

Sample Document 3.2
*Letter Notifying the Staff Member That the Impartial
Hearing Officer Recommends No Further Action Be Taken*

ABC School District

District Administration Office
Department of Personnel, Suite 117
1062 West Scott Memorial Drive
Crescent Ridge, CA 70799
(916) 444-5555

May 27, 199x

Certified Mail

Mr. William Anthony
397 West Jackson Circle
Crescent Ridge, CA 70799

Dear Mr. Anthony:

A conference was held in the Department of Personnel conference room at 1:15 p.m. on Thursday, May 23, 199x, in accordance with the provisions of Section III, Paragraph (F), of the master contract. You; Mr. Darren L. Miller, ABC Educators' Association representative; Dr. Lemmie Wade, principal of Kennedy Elementary School; and I were present at this conference.

Dr. Wade presented testimony about your using corporal punishment in your social studies class on May 18, 199x, and she included witness statements, parent complaints, and pictures showing the marks on the necks of students on the day of the incident. Dr. Wade recommended that you be suspended for six (6) consecutive school months without pay.

Mr. Darren L. Miller, ABC Educators' Association representative, presented testimony on your behalf to explain that you did not use corporal punishment. He stated that you followed procedures outlined in the master contract to prevent a breach of student discipline. He also stated that, for the past ten years, you have been a loyal employee without involvement in disciplinary incidents. In addition, he reported that you received the Elementary Teacher of the Year Award in 199x for teaching excellence. Mr. Miller recommended that all misconduct charges be dropped and all documentation relative to this incident be destroyed.

After carefully reviewing the testimony and documentation, I believe that probable cause does not exist to show that you engaged in misconduct by using corporal punishment on May 18, 199x. Insufficient evidence was provided to substantiate the charge as stated. Therefore you will receive full compensation for the time that you were suspended without pay, and all references to this misconduct will be destroyed.

Sincerely,

Dawna M. Fitzgerald, Ph.D.
Chief Personnel Director

cc: Dr. Lemmie Wade, Principal, Kennedy Elementary School
     Mr. Darren L. Miller, Representative, ABC Educators' Association

Sample Document 3.3
*Letter Notifying the Staff Member That the School
Administrator's Recommendation for Disciplinary
Action Has Been Reduced by the Impartial Hearing Officer*

ABC School District

District Administration Office
Department of Personnel, Suite 117
1062 West Scott Memorial Drive
Crescent Ridge, CA 70799
(916) 444-5555

May 27, 199x

Certified Mail

Mr. William Anthony
397 West Jackson Circle
Crescent Ridge, CA 70799

Dear Mr. Anthony:

A conference was held in the Department of Personnel conference room at 1:15 p.m. on Thursday, May 23, 199x, in accordance with the provisions of Section III, Paragraph (F), of the master contract. You; Mr. Darren L. Miller, ABC Educators' Association representative; Dr. Lemmie Wade, principal of Kennedy Elementary School; and I were present at this conference.

Dr. Wade presented testimony about you using corporal punishment in your social studies class on May 18, 199x, and she included six witness statements, three parent complaints, and five photographs showing the marks on the necks of students on the day of the incident. Dr. Wade recommended that you be suspended for six (6) consecutive school months without pay.

Mr. Darren L. Miller, ABC Educators' Association representative, presented testimony on your behalf to explain that you did not use corporal punishment. He stated that you followed procedures outlined in the master contract to prevent a breach of student discipline. He also stated that, for the past ten years, you have been a loyal employee without involvement in any disciplinary matters. In addition, he reported that you received the Elementary Teacher of the Year Award in 199x for teaching excellence.

Mr. Miller recommended that all misconduct charges be dropped because the principal had failed to prove beyond reasonable doubt that you used corporal punishment in your social studies class.

Both parties presented excellent testimony to support their case. However, I believe that probable cause exists that you engaged in misconduct by using corporal punishment in your class on May 18, 199x. Therefore I am recommending that you be suspended from the school district without pay for three (3) school days and that a letter be placed in your district personnel file.

As specified in the master contract, the ABC Educators' Association has the right to appeal this decision to the ABC School Committee of the Board of Education within ten (10) workdays.

Sincerely,

Dawna M. Fitzgerald, Ph.D.
Chief Personnel Director

cc: Dr. Lemmie Wade, Principal, Kennedy Elementary School
     Mr. Ling Yang, Director of Compensation, ABC School District
     Mr. Darren L. Miller, Representative, ABC Educators' Association

Sample Document 3.4
Letter Notifying the Staff Member That the Impartial Hearing
Officer Concurs With the School Administrator's Recommendation

ABC School District

District Administration Office
Department of Personnel, Suite 117
1062 West Scott Memorial Drive
Crescent Ridge, CA 70799
(916) 444-5555

May 29, 199x

Certified Mail

Mr. William Anthony
397 West Jackson Circle
Crescent Ridge, CA 70799

Dear Mr. Anthony:

A conference was held in the Department of Personnel conference room at 1:15 p.m. on Thursday, May 23, 199x, in accordance with the provisions of Section III, Paragraph (F), of the master contract. You; Mr. Darren L. Miller, ABC Educators' Association representative; Dr. Lemmie Wade, principal of Kennedy Elementary School; and I were present for this conference.

Dr. Wade presented testimony about your using corporal punishment in your social studies class on May 18, 199x, and she included witness statements, parent complaints, and pictures showing the marks on the necks of students on the day of the incident. Dr. Wade recommended that you be suspended for six (6) consecutive school months without pay.

Mr. Darren L. Miller, ABC Educators' Association representative, presented testimony on your behalf to explain that you did not use corporal punishment. He stated that you followed procedures outlined in the master contract to prevent a breach of student discipline. He also stated that, for the past ten years, you have been a loyal employee without any involvement in disciplinary action. In addition, he reported that you received the Elementary Teacher of the Year Award in 199x for teaching excellence. Mr. Miller recommended that all misconduct charges be dropped and any references to this incident be destroyed.

After hearing the testimony, I believe probable cause exists that you engaged in misconduct by using corporal punishment in your social studies class on May 18, 199x. Therefore I concur with Dr. Wade's recommendation. You will be suspended for six (6) school months without pay, and a copy of this letter will be placed in your district personnel file.

As specified in the master contract, you may appeal my decision to the ABC School Committee of the Board of School Directors within ten (10) workdays.

Sincerely,

Dawna M. Fitzgerald, Ph.D.
Chief Personnel Director

cc: Dr. Lemmie Wade, Principal, Kennedy Elementary School
     Mr. Ling Yang, Director of Compensation, ABC School District
     Mr. Darren L. Miller, Representative, ABC Educators' Association

Sample Document 3.5
Letter Notifying the Staff Member That a Recommendation
for Termination Is Being Sent to the Superintendent of Schools

ABC School District

District Administration Office
Department of Personnel, Suite 117
1062 West Scott Memorial Drive
Crescent Ridge, CA 70799
(916) 444-5555

May 27, 199x

Certified Mail

Mr. William Anthony
397 West Jackson Circle
Crescent Ridge, CA 70799

Dear Mr. Anthony:

A conference was held in the Department of Personnel conference room at 1:15 p.m. on Thursday, May 23, 199x, in accordance with the provisions of Section III, Paragraph (F), of the master contract. You; Mr. Darren L. Miller, ABC Educators' Association representative; Dr. Lemmie Wade, principal of Kennedy Elementary School; and I were present at this conference.

Dr. Wade presented testimony about your using corporal punishment in your social studies class on May 18, 199x, and she included witness statements, parent complaints, and pictures showing the marks on the necks of students on the day of the incident. Dr. Wade recommended that you be suspended for six (6) consecutive school months without pay.

Mr. Darren L. Miller, ABC Educators' Association representative, presented testimony on your behalf to explain that you did not use corporal punishment. He stated that you followed procedures outlined in the master contract to prevent a breach of student discipline. He also stated that, for the past ten years, you have been a loyal employee without any involvement in disciplinary action. In addition, he reported that you received the Elementary Teacher of the Year Award in 199x for teaching excellence. Mr. Miller recommended that all misconduct charges be dropped and any references to this incident be destroyed.

After hearing the testimony, I believe that probable cause exists that you engaged in misconduct by using corporal punishment in your social studies class on May 18, 199x. Because of the severity of the incident, and in view of previous warnings that have been issued to you, I am recommending to the Superintendent of Schools that you be terminated from your teaching position in the ABC School District.

As specified in the master contract, you have a right to appeal this decision to the ABC Board of Education within ten (10) workdays.

Sincerely,

Dawna M. Fitzgerald, Ph.D.
Chief Personnel Director

cc: Dr. Lemmie Wade, Principal, Kennedy Elementary School
     Mr. Ling Yang, Director of Compensation, ABC School District
     Mr. Darren L. Miller, Representative, ABC Educators' Association

Sample Document 3.6
*Letter Notifying the Staff Member That the Superintendent
of Schools Concurs With the Recommendation for Termination*

ABC School District

District Administration Office
Department of Personnel, Suite 117
1062 West Scott Memorial Drive
Crescent Ridge, CA 70799
(916) 444-5555

June 1, 199x

Certified Mail

Mr. William Anthony
397 West Jackson Circle
Crescent Ridge, CA 70799

Dear Mr. Anthony:

This letter is to inform you that I concur with the recommendation of the Super-intendent that you be terminated from your teaching position in the ABC School District. I am presenting a recommendation for your termination to the Board of Education on Friday, June 7, 199x. Section III, Paragraph (A), of the master contract outlines the procedural due process that will be followed during this hearing.

At this hearing with the Board of Education, a legal recording will be prepared. You have a right to cross-examine witnesses, decide if you wish the meeting to be open or closed to the public, and present evidence on your behalf. You are also entitled to be represented by the ABC Educators' Association or legal counsel of your choice to ensure that due process is followed according to the master contract.

After the evidence is presented at this hearing, the ABC Board of Education will make a decision relative to the recommendation for termination.

Sincerely,

Dawna M. Fitzgerald, Ph.D.
Chief Personnel Director

cc: Dr. Lemmie Wade, Principal, Kennedy Elementary School
    Mr. Darren L. Miller, Representative, ABC Educators' Association

Sample Document 3.7
Letter Notifying the Staff Member That
the Board of Education Reduced the Disciplinary Action

ABC School District   District Administration Office
                                    Department of Personnel, Suite 117
                                        1062 West Scott Memorial Drive
                                            Crescent Ridge, CA 70799
                                                    (916) 444-5555

June 12, 199x

Certified Mail

Mr. William Anthony
397 West Jackson Circle
Crescent Ridge, CA 70799

Dear Mr. Anthony:

After deliberating for six hours on the Superintendent's recommendation to terminate you from the ABC School District, the Board of Education decided to suspend you for one year without pay. Therefore you are expected to remove your personal effects from Kennedy Elementary School, plus return building keys and other school property to Dr. Lemmie Wade, principal of Kennedy Elementary School. If you do not remove your personal effects within ten (10) school days, they will be donated to a charitable organization.

Next year, you are to contact my office before August 1, 199x, to discuss re-instatement and your school assignment.

Sincerely,

Dawna M. Fitzgerald, Ph.D.
Chief Personnel Director

cc: Dr. Lemmie Wade, Principal, Kennedy Elementary School
     Mr. Ling Yang, Director of Compensation, ABC School District
     Mr. Gary P. Davis, Attorney-at-Law, Davis, Davis and Davis
     Mr. Darren L. Miller, Representative, ABC Educators' Association

Sample Document 3.8
*Letter Notifying the Staff Member That the Board
of Education Concurs With the Recommendation for Termination*

ABC School District

District Administration Office
Department of Personnel, Suite 117
1062 West Scott Memorial Drive
Crescent Ridge, CA 70799
(916) 444-5555

June 12, 199x

Certified Mail

Mr. William Anthony
397 West Jackson Circle
Crescent Ridge, CA 70799

Dear Mr. Anthony:

This letter is to inform you that the Board of Education concurs with the Superintendent's recommendation to terminate your contract. Therefore you are hereby terminated from the ABC School District.

The California State Statute, Section 2100, and the master contract as specified in Section III, Paragraph (G), are the legal basis for this action. The California State Statutes, Section 2100, state that a teacher can be terminated for unprofessional conduct, including the use of excessive corporal punishment. Also, the master contract of the ABC School District specified the provisions of misconduct to ensure that due process procedures are followed.

Please contact Mr. Ling Yang, Director of Compensation, at 444-5555 for advisement with regard to payroll or fringe benefits. Your last day of employment with the ABC School District is Monday, June 12, 199x, and your final paycheck will be sent to you by certified mail.

You are expected to remove your personal effects from the classroom and to return any keys and/or other school property to Dr. Lemmie Wade, principal at

Kennedy Elementary School. If you do not remove your personal effects within five (5) workdays, they will be donated to a community charitable organization.

Sincerely,

Dawna M. Fitzgerald, Ph.D.
Chief Personnel Director

cc: Dr. Lemmie Wade, Principal, Kennedy Elementary School
     Mr. Ling Yang, Director of Compensation, ABC School District
     Mr. Gary P. Davis, Attorney-at-Law, Davis, Davis and Davis
     Mr. Darren L. Miller, Representative, ABC Educators' Association

Misconduct Charge Statements

As a school administrator, be prepared to compromise on misconduct issues. Nothing is carved in stone.

The sample documents in this chapter list examples of misconduct charge statements. Some of the misconduct examples are serious and may require immediate suspension of the staff member from all duties with pay to allow time for you to investigate the allegations. Even though the chart does not list all misconduct charges, you should carefully review the various categories of misconduct to become familiar with the types of misconduct that may occur at school and/or involve school staff members. Additional lines are provided on the chart to allow you to add other examples of misconduct that occur in your school district.

Before reading the following chapters, you must collect historical information on dispositions that the school district rendered in the past when similar misconduct occurred. For ready reference, you should use that historical information to complete the sections on the misconduct chart. Then the completed chart will show at a glance what action was taken by the district when the first incident occurred involving the staff member and what action was taken by the district when the second incident or repeated incidents occurred involving the same staff member. When misconduct occurs, you should review the misconduct charge statement charts and then turn to the appropriate chapter in this guide.

Sample Document 4.1
Misconduct Charge Statements and
Disciplinary Action Taken for Sexually Related Misconduct

This form must be completed by the school administrator or representative for the school district.

CHARGE STATEMENT	FIRST OFFENSE	REPEATED OFFENSES
Being involved in a heterosexual act or acts with a student		
Being involved in a homosexual relationship with a student		
Describing sexual activities between adults		
Engaging in sexual harassment of female or male staff member		
Improper sexual behavior toward students		
Inappropriate sexual comments to students		
Inappropriately touching a student for sexual gratification (e.g., legs, breast, buttocks, knee, ears, back)		
Kissing a student		
Rubbing, touching, or fondling the private parts of a student		
Sexual intercourse with a student		
Sexual molestation of a student		
Sexually abusive conduct toward a student		
Showing an obscene film or X-rated film to students		
Showing pornographic materials to students		
Telling sexually related jokes to students or in the classroom		
Touching a student improperly		
Using obscene gestures toward students		
Using sexually explicit language with a student or in the classroom		
Using unapproved sexually related materials in the classroom		
Writing sexually explicit poems in class		

NOTE: See also Chapter 5.

Sample Document 4.2
Misconduct Charge Statements
and Disciplinary Action Taken for Controlled Substances

This form must be completed by the school administrator or representative for the school district.

CHARGE STATEMENT	FIRST OFFENSE	REPEATED OFFENSES
Being in possession of a controlled substance		
Being under the influence of alcohol at school		
Dealing drugs in school		
Drunkenness on the job		
Giving a controlled substance to a student		
Possession of a controlled substance in a drug-free zone		
Possession of drugs in school		
Selling a controlled substance to students		

NOTE: See also Chapter 6.

Sample Document 4.3
Misconduct Charge Statements
and Disciplinary Action Taken for Theft and Fraud

This form must be completed by the school administrator or representative for the school district.

CHARGE STATEMENT	FIRST OFFENSE	REPEATED OFFENSES
Claiming extra assignment pay on days recorded as sick		
Claiming unauthorized pay		
Claiming unauthorized sick time		
Conducting other business during school time		
Conducting personal business during school time		
Embezzling funds		
Falsifying payroll records		
Forgery		
Misappropriating school funds		
Stealing money from a staff member		
Stealing money from the school soda fund		
Stealing office supplies, books, utensils, etc.		
Taking audiovisual equipment (e.g., camcorders, radios, TV, VCR) home for personal use without authorization		
Taking computer equipment from school without authorization		
Taking unused food from the cafeteria		
Unauthorized use of federal tax exemption number		
Working for another agency during work hours		

NOTE: See also Chapter 7.

Sample Document 4.4
Misconduct Charge Statements and Disciplinary Action
Taken for Misconduct Outside the School Setting

This form must be completed by the school administrator or representative for the school district.

CHARGE STATEMENT	FIRST OFFENSE	REPEATED OFFENSES
Arrested for being involved in a car theft ring		
Arrested for being involved in an attempt to commit murder		
Arrested for being involved in armed robbery		
Arrested for exposing students to sexually sensitive materials		
Arrested for making obscene gestures with a mannequin in public		
Arrested for public lewdness		
Arrested for taking nude photographs of students		
Charged with battery		
Charged with blackmail		
Charged with burglary		
Charged with counterfeiting		
Charged with credit card fraud		
Charged with engaging in sexual activities with minors		
Charged with gross disorderly conduct		
Charged with intent to commit rape		
Charged with masturbating in a public rest room		

(continued)

CHARGE STATEMENT	FIRST OFFENSE	REPEATED OFFENSES
Charged with possession of a controlled substance (e.g., cocaine, marijuana)		
Charged with possession of stolen property		
Charged with use of explosives/firearms		

NOTE: See also Chapter 8.

Sample Document 4.5
Misconduct Charge Statements and Disciplinary Action
Taken for Abusive, Insulting, and/or Profane Language

This form must be completed by the school administrator or representative for the school district.

CHARGE STATEMENT	FIRST OFFENSE	REPEATED OFFENSES
Calling student derogatory names		
Distributing flyers with vulgar racial comments		
Making negative religious references		
Using gender slurs toward female student		
Using profanity toward school administrator in front of students		
Using profanity toward students		
Using racial slurs toward students		

NOTE: See also Chapter 9.

Sample Document 4.6
Misconduct Charge Statements
and Disciplinary Action Taken for Corporal Punishment

This form must be completed by the school administrator or representative for the school district.

CHARGE STATEMENT	FIRST OFFENSE	REPEATED OFFENSES
Causing severe injury to a student		
Hitting a student in the face		
Locking a student in a closet		
Paddling a student with a board		
Pulling a student's arm behind his or her back and holding it		
Pulling a student's hair		
Shoving a student against a wall		
Using excessive force to restrain a student		
Wrestling with a student		

NOTE: See also Chapter 10.

Sample Document 4.7
Misconduct Charge Statements
and Disciplinary Action Taken for Insubordination

This form must be completed by the school administrator or representative for the school district.

CHARGE STATEMENT	FIRST OFFENSE	REPEATED OFFENSES
Disrespect toward school administrator		
Failure to follow a reasonable directive		
Fighting with a staff member		
Gross defiance of authority		
Refusal to accept changes in teaching assignment		
Refusal to escort students to and from recess		
Refusal to leave room keys in the school office at the end of the day		
Refusal to let the school administrator into the classroom to conduct an evaluation/observation		
Refusal to meet with the principal to discuss teaching performance		
Refusal to report to class		
Refusal to teach a class		

NOTE: See also Chapter 11.

Sample Document 4.8
Misconduct Charge Statements
and Disciplinary Action Taken for Neglect of Duty

This form must be completed by the school administrator or representative for the school district.

CHARGE STATEMENT	FIRST OFFENSE	REPEATED OFFENSES
Failure to attend open house		
Failure to attend school-sponsored events		
Failure to report to duty		
Failure to submit grades on time		
Failure to supervise students		

NOTE: See also Chapter 12.

Sample Document 4.9
Misconduct Charge Statements
and Disciplinary Action Taken for Tardiness

This form must be completed by the school administrator or representative for the school district.

CHARGE STATEMENT	FIRST OFFENSE	REPEATED OFFENSES
Excessive tardiness to work		
Late to class assignment (e.g., in the teacher's lounge)		
Leaving before the end of open house		
Repeated tardiness		
Tardy 5-10 minutes to work		
Tardy 15-30 minutes to work two or more times per week		

NOTE: See also Chapter 13.

PART II

When an allegation of misconduct occurs, you should review the sample documents in Chapter 4, "Misconduct Charge Statements," to identify the misconduct category and then turn to the appropriate chapter in Part II. The chapters in Part II outline the procedures for specific categories of misconduct. However, because the examples of misconduct listed in Chapter 4 are not all-inclusive, you must select the category and chapter that best fits the situation you are investigating.

5 Sexually Related Misconduct

As a school administrator, never become romantically involved with a student or staff member.

Allegations of sexual misconduct by teachers and other staff members are a serious problem for school districts. State law defines the statutory grounds for sexually related behavior and the consequences for violating the law. In addition, the school board should have a policy stating its commitment to the professional behavior of all district employees. School districts should provide in-service activities for school administrators on conducting investigations with regard to sexually related misconduct charges against employees. It is essential that you follow an administrative procedure that coincides with the misconduct section of the master contract. As specified in the master contract, misconduct proceedings will be initiated if a staff member engages in inappropriate sexually related conduct toward a student or students.

When a student, parent, or staff member informs you about alleged inappropriate sexual incidents involving a staff member, you must act immediately to gather facts to determine if misconduct has occurred, even if the sexually related incident is the first offense or an isolated incident. Also, an allegation of sexually related misconduct is a confidential matter that affects the professional reputation of the staff member as well as creating potential financial hardship for the school district.

The allegation must be proven. That is, idle speculation does not provide the foundation for dismissal, nonrenewal of contract, and/or revocation of a teacher's license. You must show that the inappropriate sexually related misconduct has an adverse impact on the fitness of the staff member to teach or to supervise students. Therefore it is important to show that the individual is unfit to teach children in accordance with state law for dismissal and the revocation of teaching credentials. The following factors (American Law Reports, *ALR3d Cases and Annotations*, 1977, pp. 60-61) are significant in determining whether a staff member's conduct indicates unfitness to teach:

- Likelihood that the conduct may have adversely affected students or fellow teachers
- Degree of such adversity anticipated
- Proximity or remoteness of time of the conduct
- Type of teaching certificate held by the party involved
- Extenuating or aggravating circumstances, if any, surrounding the conduct
- Praiseworthiness or blameworthiness of the motives resulting in the conduct
- Likelihood of the recurrence of the questioned conduct and the extent to which disciplinary action may inflict an adverse impact or chilling effect on the constitutional rights of the staff member or other teachers involved

When allegations related to sexually related misconduct are brought to your attention, you must determine if the nature of the incident requires that the staff member be immediately suspended from all duties at the school or if you should initiate the regular misconduct procedures of the school district. If the incident requires immediate suspension of the staff member, refer to Chapter 2, "Serious Misconduct Requiring Immediate Suspension." If you decide to follow the regular misconduct procedures, however, you must still conduct a fair and objective investigation to determine if there is sufficient evidence to support the allegations. The following steps should be taken:

❑ Conduct an investigation to collect information relative to the incident.
  - Use a standard form to collect statements from the victim, all witnesses, and other individuals, including the parents, who have information about the alleged incident (e.g., students, staff, secretaries) (see Sample Document 1.6). Also, provide a diagram for the victim witnesses to identify body part(s) involved in the incident (see Sample Documents 1.7 and 1.8).
    — Remind the witnesses and victims to be specific and include the following:
      — when (date and time)
      — where (location or area)
      — who (first and last names of people involved or witnesses, if known)
      — what (events and actions)
    — Check the statements so that any inaccuracies such as date or time can be corrected by the person providing the information. If a change must be made, have the change initialed and dated by the person making the statement.
    — Interview witnesses separately and follow up with pointed questions. Probe witnesses to ensure that all information is accurate and complete.
  - Take photographs of the classroom or area where the incident occurred.
  - Take photographs of any other evidence, including the student, if marks are visible on his or her body.
  - Draw a diagram showing the location and any movement of persons involved.

- Check the school and district administration office files for previous progressive discipline information and/or misconduct letters.
- Collect any supplemental documentation (e.g., board policy relative to expected behaviors of staff members and/or relationships with students).

❑ Assess the information collected during the investigation to determine if the misconduct section of the master contract should be invoked.

❑ Send a letter to the staff member scheduling a conference to discuss the information that has come to your attention and that might lead to allegations of misconduct (see Sample Document 1.9).
  — Hold this conference as soon as possible.

❑ Prepare for the misconduct conference.
- Organize the documentation.
  — Make copies of all documentation for the staff member and the staff member's representative.
  — Make copies of students' typed statements, with the students' names omitted.
- Prepare an opening statement and use personal notes as a guide during the conference.
  — Do not give the opening statement or personal notes to the staff member or to the staff member's representative.
- Review district historical files to determine previous disciplinary action against other staff members accused of similar misconduct (see sample documents in Chapter 4, "Misconduct Charge Statements").

❑ Open the conference (see "The Misconduct Conference" section in Chapter 1, "General Misconduct Procedures").
- If individuals attending the conference do not know each other, introduce them.
- Cite the section of the master contract under which the conference is being conducted.
- Specify the sequence in which the testimony will be presented.
- If the staff member brings more than one person to the conference, ask the staff member to identify the person who will serve as his or her official representative. Other individuals should not be allowed to talk.

❑ Conduct the conference (see "The Misconduct Conference" section in Chapter 1, "General Misconduct Procedures").
- Present the case, including all documentation to support the allegations of misconduct.
- Permit the staff member and the staff member's representative to conduct a cross-examination and to present any pertinent documentation.
  — Be aware that the staff member's representative might try to put you on the defensive as a technique to justify the staff member's action, especially if you are perceived to have racial or gender or sexual orientation bias.
  — Do not interrupt; rather, let the staff member ramble.
  — Restate and clarify the comments made by the staff member.

❑ Bring closure to the conference (see "The Misconduct Conference" section in Chapter 1, "General Misconduct Procedures").

❑ After the conference, call the staff member's representative to recommend a resolution of the misconduct charge. Possible outcomes may include the following:
- If the documentation and the "preponderance of the evidence" are inadequate to support the allegation(s) that probable cause exists that misconduct

occurred, inform the staff member's representative that no further action will be taken.

- If the documentation and the "preponderance of the evidence" support the allegation(s) that probable cause exists that misconduct occurred, inform the staff member's representative about the proposed disciplinary action. If the staff member's representative refuses the resolution, move to the next step in the misconduct process, which involves an impartial hearing officer (see Chapter 3, "Presenting the Misconduct Case at a Hearing"). If the staff member's representative accepts the resolution, write the letter of reprimand (see Sample Documents 5.1 and 5.2, which represent steps 2 and 3 of progressive discipline).

- If more time is needed to deliberate, inform the staff member's representative that you will review the documentation and testimony before making a decision, following the contractual time line.

  — Recommend reasonable disciplinary action relative to the seriousness of the incident.

  — Be sure to follow consistent disciplinary action for all staff members at the school or in the school district.

Sample Document 5.1
Letter of Reprimand (1) for Sexually Related Misconduct

ABC School District

Duffy Middle School
543 Orange Drive
Crescent Ridge, CA 70799
(916) 444-3333

January 22, 199x

Certified Mail

Mr. Michael VanderMurr
482 West Valencia Court
Crescent Ridge, CA 70799

Dear Mr. VanderMurr:

This letter is an official reprimand for telling a sexually explicit joke to students in your fourth hour English classroom. On Thursday, January 11, 199x, at approximately 1:55 p.m. in Room 307 at Duffy Middle School, you allegedly told a sexual joke to female students in your class. As a result, parents of students in that class complained to the school administration. In addition, parents stated that you told female students about the type of lady that would appeal to you. You allegedly described in detail the physical features of the lady that you desired. You also said that some female students in your English class had the physical features to satisfy you sexually. This conduct is unacceptable for any staff member at Duffy Middle School.

At the first staff meeting on Monday, August 28, 199x, I discussed the Standards of Acceptable Conduct for Staff Members, and a copy of the standards, which also appears on page 2 of the Staff Handbook, was attached to the agenda. The standards are clear, direct, and unambiguous. Standard 6 states that staff members are to "refrain from any sexual conduct with students." In addition, the last sentence on the acceptable conduct list states that "If staff members fail to abide by these standards of acceptable conduct, including but not limited to the examples provided above, they may be subject to disciplinary action."

Your behavior outlined above is unacceptable at Duffy Middle School. Moreover, you must teach the English curriculum as developed by the school district, and I suggest that you review that curriculum. Also, I suggest that you read the

Staff Handbook, in particular, the Standards of Acceptable Conduct for Staff Members, keep your personal comments about females to yourself, and never direct them to students.

This official letter of reprimand is being issued to you for making inappropriate sexual comments directed to female students in your English class on January 11, 199x. You are being given an opportunity to improve your conduct. If you fail to do so, however, you will subject yourself to more severe disciplinary action. Improvement in your professional conduct is your responsibility.

If you wish to respond to this letter in writing, I must receive your response within five (5) workdays. Your statement will be attached to a copy of this letter and placed in your district personnel file.

Sincerely,

Manuel Rodriguez
Principal

cc: Dr. Dawna M. Fitzgerald, Chief Personnel Director, ABC School District
     Mr. Gary P. Davis, Attorney-at-Law, Davis, Davis and Davis
     Ms. Lucy Erickson, Representative, ABC Educators' Association

Sample Document 5.2
Letter of Reprimand (2) for Sexually Related Misconduct

ABC School District   Duffy Middle School
                                                      543 Orange Drive
                                              Crescent Ridge, CA 70799
                                                      (916) 444-3333

May 16, 199x

Certified Mail

Mr. Michael VanderMurr
482 West Valencia Court
Crescent Ridge, CA 70799

Dear Mr. VanderMurr:

This letter is an official reprimand for using unapproved sexually related materials in the classroom. On Thursday, May 9, 199x, at approximately 10:15 a.m., I personally observed you use sexually related materials in your second hour English Class. As I walked around the class, I saw students sitting at their desks reading these materials and I heard Betty Arlington, a student in the class, talking loudly and asking, "Why are we reading this nasty stuff in class?" At that point, I asked you to come into the hall to speak with you about using such materials in class. Furthermore, I told you to immediately cease using the materials. You said that the materials were part of the health education curriculum.

Ten minutes later I returned to the classroom, and you had not changed the materials. Although I gave you suggestions on how to improve your conduct, it is obvious that you did not accept them.

Later that day, I called Dr. Nathan Roberts, Director of Health Education for the ABC School District, and asked him to come to Duffy Middle School to review these materials. He stated that the materials you used in class were inappropriate for students, and he recommended that these materials be removed from your classroom and destroyed immediately.

A letter of reprimand dated January 22, 199x, was placed in your district personnel file for allegedly making inappropriate sexual comments to female students in your class. The letter further stated that you described the physical features of a female and that you stated that some female students in your English class are physically mature enough to meet your sexual needs. At that time, I warned you that you would subject yourself to more severe disciplinary action if you did not improve your conduct. It is obvious that you disregarded that first warning. Therefore this letter of reprimand and a three (3) day suspension are being given to you as a strong statement that you must correct your conduct immediately. Failure to comply with this directive will be considered insubordination and could result in severe disciplinary action up to and including termination from the ABC School District.

If you wish to respond to this letter in writing, I must receive your reply within five (5) workdays. Your statement will be attached to a copy of this letter and placed in your district personnel file.

Sincerely,

Manuel Rodriguez
Principal

cc: Dr. Dawna M. Fitzgerald, Chief Personnel Director, ABC School District
    Mr. Gary P. Davis, Attorney-at-Law, Davis, Davis and Davis
    Ms. Lucy Erickson, Representative, ABC Educators' Association

Controlled Substances

As a school administrator, never lose your temper during a misconduct hearing. Although you may be under pressure, always demonstrate self-control.

Addiction to drugs and other controlled substances by staff members is an increasing problem for school districts. In fact, many school districts have Employee Assistance Programs (EAPs) to provide confidential assistance to help staff members overcome the use of drugs or other controlled substances. Still, some staff members do not seek the assistance of such programs.

Examples of addictive substances include cocaine, marijuana, alcohol, glue, heroin, ethyl, and ethanol. Such addiction by staff members is unacceptable, and use of these substances is never tolerated in or around the school.

The school administrator must be aware of the warning signs that a staff member is under the influence of drugs or some other controlled substance. Listed below are possible warning signs that the staff member is experiencing problems:

- Mental confusion
- Memory loss
- Distorted sense of one's ability to perform assigned duties
- Undependable at work
- Violent verbal outburst around students and staff
- Loss of muscle control
- Slow speech

- Blank stare on face
- Vomiting
- Frequent colds or flu causing absenteeism and tardiness
- Runny nose
- Frequent sniffling
- Sudden weight loss
- Lying
- Stealing

School district staff members who are addicted to drugs or other controlled substances have a negative impact on the learning atmosphere in the school. Also, their absence or tardiness interferes with the effective operation of the school. Even when such staff members report to work, they are less productive in working with students and other staff. Moreover, drug-addicted staff members may ask others to cover up for them at work. If other staff members or even students do not comply, the addict often becomes hostile and bitter.

The cost to support drug or other controlled substance habits of the staff member is astronomical. Moreover, if the craving for the drug or controlled substance is not satisfied, the staff member may react angrily toward students or other staff members.

When allegations related to using a controlled substance, providing a controlled substance to students or other staff members, or being under the influence of a controlled substance are brought to your attention, you must determine if the nature of the incident requires that the staff member be suspended immediately from all duties at the school or if you should initiate the regular misconduct procedures of the school district. If the incident requires immediate suspension of the staff member, refer to Chapter 2, "Serious Misconduct Requiring Immediate Suspension." If you decide to follow the regular misconduct procedures, however, you must still conduct a fair and objective investigation to determine if there is sufficient evidence to support the allegations. The following steps should be taken:

❏ Conduct an investigation to collect information relative to the incident.
   - Use a standard form to collect statements from all witnesses and other individuals who have information about the alleged incident (e.g., students, staff, secretaries) (see Sample Document 1.6).
      — Remind the witnesses to be specific and include the following:
         — when (date and time)
         — where (location or area)
         — who (first and last names of people involved or witnesses, if known)
         — what (events and actions)
      — Check the statements so that any inaccuracies, such as date or time, can be corrected by the person providing the information. If a change must be made, have the change initialed and dated by the person making the statement.
      — Interview witnesses separately and follow up with pointed questions. Probe witnesses to ensure that all information is accurate and complete.

- Review district policies and procedures for testing the level of intoxication.
- Take photographs of the classroom or area where the incident occurred, if appropriate.
- Contact the police department and also obtain the police report and the charge statement from the district attorney's office for documentation.
- Check the school and district administration office files for previous progressive discipline information and/or misconduct letters.
- Collect any supplemental documentation (e.g., board policy relative to drug and alcohol abuse, staff handbook references, weekly bulletin references).

❑ Assess the information gathered during the investigation to determine if the misconduct section of the master contract should be invoked.

❑ Send a letter to the staff member scheduling a conference to discuss the information that has come to your attention that might lead to allegations of misconduct (see Sample Document 1.9).

— Hold this conference as soon as possible.

❑ Prepare for the misconduct conference.

- Organize the documentation.

— Make a copy of students' typed statements with the students' names omitted.

— Make copies of all documentation for the staff member and the staff member's representative.

- Review district historical records to determine previous disciplinary action against other staff members accused of similar misconduct (see sample documents in Chapter 4, "Misconduct Charge Statements").
- Prepare an opening statement and use personal notes as a guide during the conference.

— Do not give the opening statement or personal notes to the staff member or the staff member's representative.

❑ Open the conference (see "The Misconduct Conference" section in Chapter 1, "General Misconduct Procedures").

- If individuals attending the conference do not know each other, introduce them.
- Cite the section of the master contract under which the conference is being conducted.
- Specify the sequence in which the testimony will be presented.
- If the staff member brings more than one person to the conference, ask the staff member to identify the person who will serve as his or her official representative. Other individuals will not be allowed to talk.

❑ Conduct the conference (see "The Misconduct Conference" section in Chapter 1, "General Misconduct Procedures").

- Present the case, including all documentation to support the allegations of misconduct.
- Permit the staff member and the staff member's representative to conduct a cross-examination and to present any pertinent documentation.

— Be aware that the staff member's representative might try to put you on the defensive as a technique to justify the staff member's action, especially if you are perceived to have racial or gender bias.

— Do not interrupt; rather, let the staff member ramble.

— Restate and clarify the comments made by the staff member.

❑ Bring closure to the conference (see "The Misconduct Conference" section in Chapter 1, "General Misconduct Procedures").

❑ After the conference, call the staff member's representative to recommend a resolution to the misconduct charge. Possible outcomes include the following:

- If the documentation and the "preponderance of the evidence" are inadequate to support the allegation(s) that probable cause exists that misconduct occurred, inform the staff member's representative that no further action will be taken.

- If the documentation and the "preponderance of the evidence" support the allegation(s) that probable cause exists that misconduct occurred, inform the staff member's representative about the proposed disciplinary action. If the staff member's representative refuses the resolution, move to the next step in the misconduct process, which involves an impartial hearing officer (see Chapter 3, "Presenting the Misconduct at a Hearing"). If the staff member's representative accepts the resolution, write the letter of reprimand (see Sample Documents 6.1 and 6.2, which represent steps 2 and 3 of progressive discipline).

- If more time is needed to deliberate, inform the staff member's representative that you will review the documentation and testimony before making a decision, following the contractual time line.

  — Recommend reasonable disciplinary action relative to the seriousness of the incident.

  — Be sure that consistent disciplinary action is followed for all staff members at the school or in the school district.

Sample Document 6.1
Letter of Reprimand (1) for Controlled Substances

ABC School District

Estrada High School
1955 Orchard Road
Crescent Ridge, CA 70799
(916) 444-2222

October 4, 199x

Certified Mail

Ms. Inez Bartlain
871 Park Lane
Crescent Ridge, CA 70799

Dear Ms. Bartlain:

This letter of reprimand is being issued to you for being under the influence of alcohol at school. After lunch on Wednesday, September 27, 199x, at approximately 1:25 p.m., you were in your science classroom during the fifth hour, teaching what appeared to be an incoherent lesson on soil erosion. My assistant principal, Ms. Gloria Jennings, informed me that students in your class said they smelled alcohol on your breath. Ms. Jennings also informed me that your room had a strong odor of alcohol. As a result, I went to your room, arranged for another teacher to cover your class, and escorted you to my office, where I informed you that you had been accused of teaching in a very incoherent manner and having a smell of alcohol on your breath. You tried to respond; however, your language was slow and you were unable to justify your speech pattern. In addition, your breath had a very strong alcohol odor. When I asked if you had been drinking during your lunch hour, you said, "No." After I questioned you further, you stated, "I had two beers in the restaurant."

Ms. Bartlain, on August 23, 199x—the first day of school—I distributed copies of the Standards of Acceptable Conduct for Staff Members. These standards are clear, direct, and unambiguous, and Standard 8 specifically states that staff members are to "refrain from coming to work under the influence of alcohol/drugs or being in possession of a controlled substance."

On September 8, 199x, I informed you that I had heard rumors that you were teaching under the influence of alcohol. At that time, I gave you a strong oral reprimand, clearly informing you that such behavior is unacceptable for staff members and that you would subject yourself to disciplinary action if you were at work under the influence of alcohol or drugs. Also, I strongly suggested that you seek assistance through the district's voluntary Employee Assistance Program.

This letter serves as an official reprimand for being under the influence of alcohol at work on September 27, 199x. I hope that you will improve your conduct; however, if you fail to correct your behavior, you will be subject to more severe disciplinary action. The ultimate responsibility to improve your conduct rests with you.

If you wish to respond to this letter in writing, I must receive your response within five (5) workdays. Your statement will be attached to this letter and placed in your district personnel file.

Sincerely,

Benjamin Najam
Principal

cc: Dr. Dawna M. Fitzgerald, Chief Personnel Director, ABC School District
     Mr. Samuel Denison, Representative, ABC Educators' Association

Sample Document 6.2
Letter of Reprimand (2) With
Suspension for Controlled Substances

ABC School District

Estrada High School
1955 Orchard Road
Crescent Ridge, CA 70799
(916) 444-2222

February 14, 199x

Certified Mail

Ms. Inez Bartlain
871 Park Lane
Crescent Ridge, CA 70799

Dear Ms. Bartlain:

This second letter of reprimand is being issued to you for coming to work under the influence of alcohol. At 9:20 a.m. on Monday, February 12, 199x, students from your first hour class came to my office and informed me that they smelled alcohol on your breath while you were teaching. Also, the students reported that you fell asleep at your desk while they were reading their textbooks and that you were unable to walk around the classroom without stumbling. I went to your classroom and found you sleeping at your desk during your preparation period. I escorted you to my office and contacted Ms. Gloria Johnson, my assistant principal, as well as Mr. Leroy Morgan, representative for the ABC Educators' Association. When they arrived, they also witnessed your physical condition and your incoherent speech.

This is the third time that I have informed you about this problem. Specifically, on September 8, 199x, I issued an oral reprimand to you and told you about the rumor that you were teaching while under the influence of alcohol. I reviewed with you the Standards of Acceptable Conduct and read item 8, which states that staff members are to "refrain from coming to work under the influence of alcohol/drugs or being in possession of a controlled substance." Then on October 4, 199x, I issued you a letter of reprimand for being under the influence of alcohol at school and suggested that you seek assistance through the district's Employee Assistance Program. Also, I reminded you that you were responsible for educating your students in an environment free of alcohol use by a staff member. I again recommended that you seek assistance from the district's Employee Assistance Program because it was obvious that you had not followed my previous recommendation.

This letter serves as an official reprimand for being under the influence of alcohol at work on February 12, 199x. I am recommending that you be suspended for three (3) days without pay. If you fail to correct your conduct, you may subject yourself to more severe disciplinary action up to and including termination.

If you wish to respond to this letter in writing, I must receive your response within five (5) workdays. Your statement will be attached to this letter and placed in your district personnel file.

Sincerely,

Benjamin Najam
Principal

cc: Dr. Dawna M. Fitzgerald, Chief Personnel Director, ABC School District
     Mr. Samuel Denison, Representative, ABC Educators' Association

7

Theft and Fraud

As the school administrator, you must set a good example of acceptable conduct for the staff. If you do something wrong, your staff will know about it.

Theft of school property or funds and fraud committed against the school district deprive students and staff members of resources that could be used to improve their learning opportunities. Expanded use of technology in schools has increased the school district's investment in a variety of new high-tech school equipment, including VCRs, laser discs, computers, laser printers, camcorders, televisions, and cameras. Because of the value of these items, schools must take measures to inventory and protect this equipment from thieves who break into the school to steal such items. The school must also protect itself against staff members who take equipment home for personal use without the authorization of the school administrator.

The staff member taking the equipment may not have any intention of returning it to the school. Students suffer the hardship of being denied the opportunity to use equipment purchased with the school district's funds to enhance the learning environment and improve the quality of their education.

When the distributor sends the equipment to the school, the administrator must have procedures to verify the purchase order, inventory the equipment received, label the equipment with the district logo, and assign an identification number. The school administrator must also keep excellent records of equipment purchased for the school, including the requisition order number, date ordered, model number of the equipment, price of equipment, and quantity ordered. Most important, the school administrator should take photographs or videotape high-tech equipment such as computers, shop equipment, VCRs, disc players, TVs, and cameras.

When allegations related to theft or fraud are brought to your attention, you must determine if the nature of the incident requires immediate suspension from all duties at the school or if you should initiate the regular misconduct procedures of the school district. If the incident requires immediate suspension of the staff member, refer to Chapter 2, "Serious Misconduct Requiring Immediate Suspension." If you decide to follow the regular misconduct procedures, however, you must still conduct a fair and objective investigation to determine if there is sufficient evidence to support the allegations. The following steps should be taken:

❑ Conduct an investigation to collect information relative to the incident.
  • Use a standard form to collect statements from all witnesses who have information about the alleged incident (see Sample Document 1.6).
  • Take photographs of or videotape any other evidence.
  • Check the school and district administration office files for previous progressive discipline information and/or misconduct letters.
  • Collect any supplemental documentation (e.g., board policy relative to fundraising, staff handbook references such as Guidelines for Taking School Owned Property Away from the School, weekly bulletin references).
❑ Report the incident to district administration and the appropriate community agency.
  • Obtain a copy of inventory slips to determine the purchase prices and quantity ordered.
  • Complete district forms (e.g., a theft/missing property report).
  • Call the police to file a theft report.
  • Inform the district insurance manager about the theft.
❑ Assess the information gathered during the investigation to determine if the misconduct section of the master contract should be invoked.
❑ Send a letter to the staff member scheduling a conference to discuss the information that has come to your attention that might lead to allegations of misconduct (see Sample Document 1.9).
  — Hold this conference as soon as possible.
❑ Prepare for the misconduct conference.
  • Organize the documentation and make copies of all documentation for the staff member and the staff member's representative.
  • Review district historical records to determine previous disciplinary action against other staff members accused of similar misconduct (see sample documents in Chapter 4, "Misconduct Charge Statements").
  • Prepare an opening statement and personal notes to use as a guide during the conference.
    — Do not give the opening statement or personal notes to the staff member or the staff member's representative.
❑ Open the conference (see "The Misconduct Conference" section in Chapter 1, "General Misconduct Procedures").

- If individuals do not know each other, introduce them.
- Cite the section of the master contract under which the conference is being conducted.
- Specify the sequence in which the testimony will be presented.
- If the staff member brings more than one person to the conference, ask the staff member to identify the person who will serve as his or her official representative. Other individuals will not be allowed to talk.

❑ Conduct the conference (see "The Misconduct Conference" section in Chapter 1, "General Misconduct Procedures").

- Present the case, including all documentation to support the allegations of misconduct.
- Permit the staff member and the staff member's representative to conduct a cross-examination and to present any pertinent documentation.
  —Be aware that the staff member's representative might try to put you on the defensive as a technique to justify the staff member's action, especially if you are perceived to have racial or gender bias.
  —Do not interrupt; rather, let the staff member ramble.
  —Restate and clarify the comments made by the staff member.

❑ Bring closure to the conference (see "The Misconduct Conference" section in Chapter 1, "General Misconduct Procedures").

❑ After the conference, call the staff member's representative to recommend a resolution of the misconduct charge. Possible outcomes include the following:

- If the documentation and the "preponderance of the evidence" are inadequate to support the allegation(s) that probable cause exists that misconduct occurred, inform the staff member's representative that no further action will be taken.
- If the documentation and the "preponderance of the evidence" support the allegation(s) that probable cause exists that misconduct occurred, inform the staff member's representative about the proposed disciplinary action. If the staff member's representative refuses the resolution, move to the next step of the misconduct process, which involves an impartial hearing officer (see Chapter 3, "Presenting the Misconduct Case at a Hearing"). If the staff member's representative accepts the resolution, write the letter of reprimand (see Sample Documents 7.1 and 7.2, which represent steps 2 and 3 of progressive discipline).
- If more time is needed to deliberate, inform the staff member's representative that you will review the documentation and testimony before making a decision, following the contractual time line.
  —Recommend reasonable disciplinary action relative to the seriousness of the incident.
  —Be sure that consistent disciplinary action is followed for all staff members at the school or in the school district.

Sample Document 7.1
Letter of Reprimand (1) for Theft or Fraud

ABC School District   Kennedy Elementary School
                                                         1584 South Pineview Drive
                                                         Crescent Ridge, CA 70799
                                                              (916) 444-8888

May 10, 199x

Certified Mail

Mr. William Anthony
397 West Jackson Circle
Crescent Ridge, CA 70799

Dear Mr. Anthony:

This letter of reprimand is being issued to you for theft of money collected from students. During January, February, and March 199x, your students participated in a fund-raiser to earn money to pay for their spring break field trip to Washington, D.C. You did not follow fund-raising procedures, however, as specified on page 42 of the Staff Handbook. In early October 199x, you requested field trip forms and an application for an extended field trip that specified the district's procedures for collecting and depositing field trip money as well as a fund-raiser application form. The completed fund-raiser form that you submitted showed that you planned to take your sixth-grade students to Washington, D.C., during the spring break. According to records from the fund-raiser organization that you worked with, the profits were $5,245. But the financial records of the school accountant show that you deposited only $4,010 for the extended field trip.

As specified in the Staff Handbook, staff members conducting a fund-raising activity are to deposit on a daily basis to the school accountant all money collected from students and receive a receipt for the funds from the accountant. You did not deposit any funds into the school's extended field trip account during February 199x. On Monday, March 4, 199x, I asked you for all documentation relative to the fund-raiser and your Washington, D.C., field trip account. At that time, you stated you could account for all funds and that you had money in a locked drawer of your desk.

Mr. Anthony, I must again inform you that all staff members are to follow the procedures for extended field trips and fund-raising. All funds must be accounted for as specified on the application forms. Attached are a copy of the extended field trip procedures, a copy of the fund-raising procedures, and a copy of procedures for handling money from the school Financial Manual. I want to state as emphatically as possible that you must obey all rules for handling school money.

This letter serves as an official reprimand for failure to follow the procedures for fund-raising and extended field trips. You are being given another chance to comply with the extended field trip and fund-raising procedures of the school. I hope you will take advantage of this opportunity to correct your conduct. If you fail to abide by the procedures and guidelines as outlined in this letter, you will be subject to further disciplinary action.

If you wish to respond to this letter in writing, I must receive your response within five (5) workdays. Your statement will be attached to a copy of this letter and placed in your district personnel file.

Sincerely,

Lemmie Wade, Ph.D.
Principal

cc: Dr. Dawna M. Fitzgerald, Chief Personnel Director, ABC School District
Mr. Darren L. Miller, Representative, ABC Educators' Association

Sample Document 7.2
Letter of Reprimand (2) With
Suspension for Theft or Fraud

ABC School District   Kennedy Elementary School
                                              1584 South Pineview Drive
                                              Crescent Ridge, CA 70799
                                                  (916) 444-8888

February 14, 199x

Certified Mail

Mr. William Anthony
397 West Jackson Circle
Crescent Ridge, CA 70799

Dear Mr. Anthony:

This letter of reprimand is being issued to you for removing school equipment without my authorization. On June 8, 199x, you took home a Macintosh computer and a laser printer valued at over $6,600. Even though staff members are permitted to take computer equipment home during the summer, they must complete an official release statement that is signed by me. Furthermore, all school equipment must be returned to the school at the beginning of the academic year so that it is available for student use.

On Thursday, August 25, 199x, which was the first day of school, all staff members were informed of the procedures for taking school equipment out of the building. In addition, a copy of the Standards of Acceptable Conduct for staff members was distributed to all staff members. These standards are clear, direct, and unambiguous. Standard 11 states that staff members are to "refrain from removing any school-owned equipment or supplies without the written authorization of the principal." The Standards of Acceptable Conduct are also listed on page 39 of the Staff Handbook.

On Monday, September 11, 199x, I asked you about the computer equipment missing from your classroom. You stated that you had taken it home and would return it the next day. I reminded you about the procedures for removing school equipment from school and directed you to read the Staff Handbook section outlining the procedures.

Therefore this letter serves as a reprimand for failure to follow school procedure for removing school equipment without authorization. Although you were given a chance to improve your unprofessional conduct in another incident, you have failed to make corrections. Therefore I am recommending that you be suspended for one (1) day without pay. If there are any further incidents, you will subject yourself to more severe disciplinary action up to and including termination from the ABC School District.

You may wish to respond to this letter in writing. I must receive your response within five (5) workdays. Your statement will be attached to a copy of this letter and will be placed in your district personnel file.

Sincerely,

Lemmie Wade, Ph.D.
Principal

cc: Dr. Dawna M. Fitzgerald, Chief Personnel Director, ABC School District
     Mr. Darren L. Miller, Representative, ABC Educators' Association

8 Misconduct Outside the School Setting

As a school administrator, avoid social relationships with staff members.

Because staff members are role models for children in and outside of the school setting, they are held to a higher standard of conduct than are other individuals. In fact, school staff members are expected to behave in such a way that they would not set a bad example for students, and can be dismissed if sufficient evidence indicates that there is the potential that they might engage in related misconduct with a student or if their outside conduct has gained sufficient notoriety that it would impair their on-the-job effectiveness or their working relationships with staff, students, and parents (Dismissal, 78ALR3d19, p. 48). "Incapacity to teach can be established by finding that the staff member would have an adverse effect on the student in the classroom" (American Law Reports, *ALR3d Cases and Annotations*, 1977, p. 54).

When a staff member is involved in unacceptable conduct outside the school setting, the incident may result in allegations of misconduct. The unacceptable conduct of a staff member is usually serious enough that it involves the police department or other law enforcement agencies with arrest powers. The allegation of misconduct against the staff member may involve serious charges for involvement in an incident such as armed robbery, car theft, illegal drug possession or use, possession of stolen items, murder, or sexual activity involving minor children. The staff member may be formally arrested on charges and required to appear in court. In some instances, the staff member may be incarcerated for a period of time, and the school district may be required to postpone the misconduct process until the staff member can attend the misconduct conference.

When allegations related to inappropriate conduct outside the school setting are brought to your attention, you must determine if the nature of the incident requires that the staff member be suspended immediately or if you should initiate the regular misconduct procedures of the school district. If the incident requires immediate suspension of the staff member, refer to Chapter 2, "Serious Misconduct Requiring Immediate Suspension." If you decide to follow the regular misconduct procedures, however, you must still conduct a fair and objective investigation to determine if there is sufficient evidence to support the allegations. The following steps should be taken:

❑ Conduct an investigation to collect information relative to the incident.
- Contact the law enforcement agencies involved (e.g., police, sheriff, FBI, Department of Social Services) for their reports and the charge statement.
- Collect any supplemental documentation (e.g., staff member's original application for employment, background check).
- Check the school and district administration office files for previous progressive discipline information and/or misconduct letters.

❑ Assess the information obtained from the law enforcement agency during the investigation to determine if the misconduct section of the master contract should be invoked.

❑ Send a letter to the staff member scheduling a conference to discuss the allegations of serious misconduct (see Sample Document 1.9).
— Hold this conference as soon as possible.

❑ Prepare for the misconduct conference.
- Make copies of all documentation for the staff member and the staff member's representative.
- Review district historical files to determine previous disciplinary action against other staff members accused of similar misconduct (see sample documents in Chapter 4, "Misconduct Charge Statements").
- Prepare an opening statement and personal notes to use as a guide during the conference.
— Do not give the opening statement or personal notes to the staff member or the staff member's representative.

❑ Open the conference (see "The Misconduct Conference" section in Chapter 1, "General Misconduct Procedures").
- If individuals attending the conference do not know each other, introduce them.
- Cite the section of the master contract under which the conference is being conducted.
- Specify the sequence in which the testimony will be presented.
- If the staff member brings more than one person to the conference, ask the staff member to identify the person who will serve as his or her official representative. Other individuals will not be allowed to talk.

❑ Conduct the conference (see "The Misconduct Conference" section in Chapter 1, "General Misconduct Procedures").

- Present the case, including all documentation to support the allegations of misconduct.
- Permit the staff member and the staff member's representative to conduct a cross-examination and to present any pertinent documentation.
    — Be aware that the staff member's representative might try to put you on the defensive as a technique to justify the staff member's action, especially if the representative perceives that you have racial or gender bias.
    — Do not interrupt; rather, let the staff member ramble.
    — Restate and clarify the comments made by the staff member. Bring closure to the conference (see "The Misconduct Conference" section in Chapter 1, "General Misconduct Procedures").

❑ After the conference, call the staff member's representative to recommend a resolution for the misconduct charge. Possible outcomes include the following:

- If the documentation and the "preponderance of the evidence" are inadequate to support the allegation(s) that probable cause exists that misconduct occurred, inform the staff member's representative that no further action will be taken.
- If the documentation and the "preponderance of the evidence" support the allegation(s) that probable cause exists that misconduct occurred, inform the staff member's representative about the proposed disciplinary action. If the staff member's representative refuses the resolution, move to the next step of the misconduct process, which involves an impartial hearing officer (see Chapter 3, "Presenting the Misconduct Case at a Hearing"). If the staff member's representative accepts the resolution, write the letter of reprimand (see Sample Documents 8.1 and 8.2, which represent steps 2 and 3 of progressive discipline).
- If more time is needed to deliberate, inform the staff member's representative that you will review the documentation and testimony before making a decision, following the contractual time line.
    — Recommend reasonable disciplinary action relative to the seriousness of the incident.
    — Be sure that consistent disciplinary action is followed for all staff members at the school or in the school district.

Sample Document 8.1
Letter of Reprimand (1) for
Misconduct Outside the School Setting

ABC School District

Kennedy Elementary School
1584 South Pineview Drive
Crescent Ridge, CA 70799
(916) 444-8888

December 2, 199x

Certified Mail

Mr. William Anthony
397 West Jackson Circle
Crescent Ridge, CA 70799

Dear Mr. Anthony:

In compliance with Section III, paragraph (A), of the master contract, a conference was held in my office on Monday, December 1, 199x, relative to allegations of misconduct. You, Mr. Darren L. Miller of the ABC Educators' Association, and I were present at this meeting. At that time we discussed your arrest and court arraignment.

You stated that you were released on bail and that a court date is pending. You also stated that the incident occurred when you were approached by your former girlfriend and her new boyfriend at a dance. An argument started and, to protect yourself, you fought with the new boyfriend. The police arrested you, your ex-girlfriend, and her new boyfriend.

Although disorderly conduct is a misdemeanor charge, you are in a position of trust and influence over students. You serve as a role model for students; therefore your behavior is held to a higher standard than that set for other individuals. Fighting is unacceptable behavior for a professional educator. You set examples for your students even when you are in the community.

This letter serves as an official reprimand for unprofessional conduct outside the school setting. If there are further incidents of disorderly conduct outside or inside the school setting, you will be subject to further disciplinary action.

If you wish to respond to this letter in writing, I must receive your response within five (5) workdays. Your statement will be attached to this letter and placed in your district personnel file.

Sincerely,

Lemmie Wade, Ph.D.
Principal

cc: Dr. Dawna M. Fitzgerald, Chief Personnel Director, ABC School District
     Mr. Darren L. Miller, Representative, ABC Educators' Association

Sample Document 8.2
*Letter of Reprimand (2) With Suspension
for Misconduct Outside the School Setting*

ABC School District

Kennedy Elementary School
1584 South Pineview Drive
Crescent Ridge, CA 70799
(916) 444-8888

May 9, 199x

Certified Mail

Mr. William Anthony
397 West Jackson Circle
Crescent Ridge, CA 70799

Dear Mr. Anthony:

This is the second letter of reprimand issued to you for misconduct outside the school setting. On Wednesday, March 27, 199x, a conference was held in my office to discuss allegations of misconduct against you for disorderly conduct at a dance. You, Mr. Darren L. Miller of the ABC Educators' Association, and I were present at this meeting. At that time, I stated that you, as a teacher, are a role model and held to a higher standard of behavior than other individuals in the community. Also, I told you that you would be subject to more severe disciplinary action if you were involved in future disorderly conduct incidents.

On May 5, 199x, you were again arrested and charged with disorderly conduct and battery against the new boyfriend of your previous girlfriend. Therefore I held a conference with you on Wednesday, May 8, 199x, to discuss the allegations of misconduct. Also present was Mr. Darren L. Miller, ABC Educators' Association. During the conference, I stated the charge and presented testimony regarding this incident as well as reading the official police report.

In response, you stated that you were again approached by your ex-girlfriend's boyfriend and were again forced to defend yourself. Yet, the police report stated that you were the aggressor and attacked the victim with intent to cause him bodily harm. Moreover, he was taken to the emergency hospital with severe lacerations around his head, neck, and shoulder areas. Your statement and the police report are entirely different.

Mr. Anthony, I must remind you again that your position in the school and the school district places a higher standard upon your conduct. In fact, your conduct in both situations was unacceptable for a professional educator.

This letter serves as an official reprimand for misconduct outside the school, and I am recommending that you be suspended for five (5) workdays without pay. Also, I want to clearly state that you subject yourself to severe disciplinary action up to and including termination from the ABC School District if you are involved in any future incidents of misconduct outside the school. You are ultimately responsible for improving your conduct.

If you wish to respond to this letter in writing, I must receive your response within five (5) workdays. Your statement will be attached to this letter and placed in your district personnel file.

Sincerely,

Lemmie Wade, Ph.D.
Principal

cc: Dr. Dawna M. Fitzgerald, Chief Personnel Director, ABC School District
     Mr. Darren L. Miller, Representative, ABC Educators' Association

$\mathcal{9}$ Abusive, Insulting, and/or Profane Language

As the school administrator, you must protect our most precious resources—our children—from staff members who commit misconduct.

Schools must ensure that our most precious resources—our children—are educated in a safe and nurturing environment without fear and intimidation caused by staff members. Although some students come to school with problems, there is no excuse for any staff member using abusive and insulting language toward them. Quite frankly, it is unacceptable conduct for any staff members to use insulting, abusive, and/or profane language toward children, regardless of their socioeconomic status or racial identity. Abusive and insulting statements can, and frequently do, cause psychological damage in the form of emotional pain and/or bitterness. Thus children must be protected against verbal abuse by staff members.

When a staff member directs abusive and insulting language toward students, you must deal quickly with the situation. Regardless of a student's background and home environment, the school setting should be a place where the student can find acceptance.

When allegations related to using abusive, insulting, and/or profane language toward students are brought to your attention, you must determine if the nature of the incident requires immediate suspension of the staff member from all duties at the school or if you should initiate the regular misconduct procedures of the school district. If the incident requires immediate suspension of the staff member, refer to Chapter 2, "Serious Misconduct Requiring Immediate Suspension." If you decide to follow the regular misconduct procedures, however, you must still conduct a fair and objective investigation to determine if there is sufficient evidence to support the allegations. The following steps should be taken:

❑ Conduct an investigation to collect information relative to the incident.
  • Use a standard form to collect statements from all witnesses and other individuals, including the parents, who have information about the alleged incident (e.g., students, staff, secretaries) (see Sample Document 1.6).
    — Remind the witnesses and victims to be specific and include the following:
      — when (date and time)
      — where (location or area)
      — who (first and last names of people involved or witnesses, if known)
      — what (events and actions)
    — Check the statements so that any inaccuracies, such as date or time, can be corrected by the person providing the information. If a change must be made, have the change initialed and dated by the person making the statement.
    — Interview witnesses separately and follow up with pointed questions. Probe witnesses to ensure that all information is accurate and complete.
  • Check the school and district administration office files for previous progressive discipline information and/or misconduct letters.
  • Collect any supplemental documentation (e.g., board policy relative to professional behavior of staff members, staff handbook references such as "Tips for Reducing Staff/Student Conflicts," weekly bulletin references).
❑ Assess the information collected during the investigation to determine if the misconduct section of the master contract should be invoked.
❑ Send a letter to the staff member scheduling a conference to discuss the information that has come to your attention that might lead to allegations of misconduct (see Sample Document 1.9).
  — Hold this conference as soon as possible.
❑ Prepare for the misconduct conference.
  • Organize the documentation.
    — Make a copy of students' typed statements, with the students' names omitted.
    — Make copies of all documentation for the staff member and the staff member's representative.
  • Review district historical records to determine previous disciplinary action against other staff members accused of similar misconduct (see sample documents in Chapter 4, "Misconduct Charge Statements").
  • Prepare an opening statement and personal notes to use as a guide during the conference.
    — Do not give the opening statement or personal notes to the staff member or the staff member's representative.
❑ Open the conference (see "The Misconduct Conference" section in Chapter 1, "General Misconduct Procedures").
  • If the individuals attending the conference do not know each other, introduce them.

- Cite the section of the master contract under which the conference is being conducted.
- Specify the sequence in which the testimony will be presented.
- If the staff member brings more than one person to the conference, ask the staff member to identify the person who will serve as his or her official representative. Other individuals will not be allowed to talk.

❏ Conduct the conference (see "The Misconduct Conference" section in Chapter 1, "General Misconduct Procedures").

- Present the case, including all documentation to support the allegations of misconduct.
- Permit the staff member and the staff member's representative to conduct a cross-examination and to present any pertinent documentation.
  - Be aware that the staff member's representative might try to put you on the defensive as a technique to justify the action, especially if you are perceived to have racial or gender bias.
  - Do not interrupt; rather, let the staff member ramble.
  - Restate and clarify the comments made by the staff member.

❏ Bring closure to the conference (see "The Misconduct Conference" section in Chapter 1, "General Misconduct Procedures").

❏ After the conference, call the staff member's representative to recommend a resolution of the misconduct charge. Possible outcomes include the following:

- If the documentation and the "preponderance of the evidence" are inadequate to support the allegation(s) that probable cause exists that misconduct occurred, inform the staff member's representative that no further action will be taken.
- If the documentation and the "preponderance of the evidence" support the allegation(s) that probable cause exists that misconduct occurred, inform the staff member's representative about the proposed disciplinary action. If the representative refuses the resolution, move to the next step of the misconduct process, which involves an impartial hearing officer (see Chapter 3, "Presenting the Misconduct Case at a Hearing"). If the staff member's representative accepts the resolution, write the letter of reprimand (see Sample Documents 9.1 and 9.2, which represent steps 2 and 3 of progressive discipline).
- If more time is needed to deliberate, inform the staff member's representative that you will review the documentation and testimony before making a decision, following the contractual time line.
  - Recommend reasonable disciplinary action relative to the seriousness of the incident.
  - Be sure that consistent disciplinary action is followed for all staff members at the school or in the school district.

Sample Document 9.1
Letter of Reprimand (1) for Abusive,
Insulting, and/or Profane Language

ABC School District   Duffy Middle School
                                                       543 Orange Drive
                                                   Crescent Ridge, CA 70799
                                                       (916) 444-3333

October 18, 199x

Certified Mail

Mr. Michael VanderMurr
482 West Valencia Court
Crescent Ridge, CA 70799

Dear Mr. VanderMurr:

This letter is to reprimand you for using abusive and insulting language toward children in your reading and language arts class on Friday, September 8, 199x, at approximately 9:54 a.m. Five parents formally complained to me on Monday, September 11, 199x, about you referring to students in your class as a "bunch of dumb asses." Statements from students in your class also indicate that you called the class a "bunch of dumb asses." Although you denied using that language, I verbally warned you that using abusive and insulting language was unacceptable conduct for a staff member. At that conference, I also gave you another copy of the Standards of Acceptable Conduct for Staff Members and reminded you that these standards are clear, direct, and unambiguous. Standard 7 specifically states that staff members are "to refrain from using abusive, insulting, and/or profane language toward students."

Because allegations of your using abusive and insulting language toward students have continued in spite of my warnings, a misconduct conference was held in my office on Tuesday, October 17, 199x. Ms. Lucy Erickson, ABC Educators' Association representative, was also present at this conference. We discussed a situation that occurred on Thursday, October 12, 199x, in which parents complained that you used abusive and insulting language directed toward their children. At the conference, you again stated that you did not use abusive language toward your students. Although you denied the allegation of using abusive language toward students, I told you to review the disciplinary procedures in the staff handbook and develop strategies to improve your conduct and cease using abusive and insulting language toward students in your classroom.

This letter serves as an official reprimand for using abusive and insulting language toward students in your classroom. If you fail to correct your conduct, you will subject yourself to further disciplinary action.

If you wish to respond to this letter in writing, I must receive your response within five (5) workdays. Your statement will be attached to a copy of this letter and placed in your district personnel file.

Sincerely,

Manuel Rodriguez
Principal

cc: Dr. Dawna M. Fitzgerald, Chief Personnel Director, ABC School District
     Ms. Lucy Erickson, Representative, ABC Educators' Association

Sample Document 9.2
Letter of Reprimand (2) With Suspension
for Abusive, Insulting, and/or Profane Language

ABC School District

Duffy Middle School
543 Orange Drive
Crescent Ridge, CA 70799
(916) 444-3333

February 14, 199x

Certified Mail

Mr. Michael VanderMurr
482 West Valencia Court
Crescent Ridge, CA 70799

Dear Mr. VanderMurr:

This letter is the second official reprimand issued to you for using abusive and insulting language toward children. Parents of students in your class complained again that you called students abusive and insulting names in your science class on Tuesday, February 7, 199x, at approximately 2:14 p.m. To be specific, you allegedly called your students "a group of monkey ass kids." Statements from students showed that you called them an insulting name.

I warned you verbally about using abusive and insulting language toward children on Friday, September 11, 199x. I told you that I had received information from students and parents that you used abusive and insulting language by making negative religious statements toward certain children in your class. At that conference, I gave you an opportunity to discuss your view of the allegations that were made against you. I also verbally warned you that using such language is not consistent with the Standards of Acceptable Conduct for Staff Members. Standard 7 specifically states that staff members must "refrain from using abusive, insulting, and/or profane language toward students."

I held a formal misconduct conference with you in my office on Tuesday, October 17, 199x, about your using abusive and insulting language in your class. You were represented at this conference by Ms. Lucy Erickson of the ABC Educators' Association. We discussed a statement that substantiated that you used abusive and insulting language in your classroom on Friday, September 8, Monday,

September 11, and Thursday, October 12, 199x. I told you that you would be subject to further disciplinary action if your conduct did not improve. The first written letter of reprimand was placed in your personnel file.

This letter is an official reprimand for using abusive and insulting language toward students in your classroom. As a resolution of this misconduct, I am recommending that you be suspended for three (3) days without pay. I hope that you will consider the seriousness of this letter of reprimand and that you will take the necessary action to stop using abusive and insulting language in the classroom. If you fail to improve your behavior, you will be subject to severe disciplinary action up to and including termination from the ABC School District. You are ultimately responsible for improving your conduct.

If you wish to respond to this letter in writing, I must receive your response within five (5) workdays. Your statement will be attached to a copy of this letter and placed in your district personnel file.

Sincerely,

Manuel Rodriguez
Principal

cc: Dr. Dawna M. Fitzgerald, Personnel Director, ABC School District
    Ms. Lucy Erickson, Representative, ABC Educators' Association

10 Corporal Punishment

As a school administrator, never violate the misconduct section of the master contract.

When children are in the school setting, their care and well-being are the responsibility of the school staff. School staffs serve *in loco parentis,* or in the place of the parent. Some states have interpreted this to mean that school staff can discipline students as the need arises, including the use of corporal punishment. Corporal punishment means the intentional infliction of physical pain that is used as a means of discipline.

Under the common law, a staff member has the right to administer reasonable corporal punishment, which may include paddling or causing some form of discomfort to the student's body (Reutter, 1985, p. 695). Some states have statutes that approve the use of that form of punishment under specified conditions (Reutter, 1985, p. 694). Unless restricted by state law, school boards generally have the authority to adopt policies controlling the use of corporal punishment. Most often, however, the courts sustain the dismissal of teachers who use corporal punishment in defiance of administrative directives (Delon, 1977, p. 39). In addition to school board action that may lead to the staff member's discharge, unreasonable corporal punishment can be the basis for a civil and/or criminal charge of assault and battery (Reutter, 1985, p. 696). The punishment given to a student by a staff member must be in proportion to the seriousness of the offense and the characteristics of the student involved (e.g., gender, age, size as well as mental, emotional, and physical condition; Reutter, 1985, p. 694). In addition, if the staff member did not intend to injure or did not administer the punishment with a reckless disregard of consequences, he or she generally will not be held liable. In most states and according to board policy in many school districts, inflicting pain for the purpose of student discipline is in clear violation of the laws. Therefore you must provide staff members with clear guidelines relative to the use of corporal punishment as well as present alternatives to correcting disruptive behavior that may precipitate a confrontational situation between a staff member and a student. You should provide staff members with strategies for dealing with their own temper so they will know when and how to stop an incident.

To reduce the potential for the use of corporal punishment, you must discuss your expectations for behavior of staff members and acceptable disciplinary techniques at the beginning of the school year. Also, you should provide teachers with tips for reducing student-staff confrontations and encourage teachers to attend in-services on classroom management and behavioral modification.

Reasonable force can be used to protect a student or restrain a student. Teachers working with emotionally disturbed students and/or other students who may exhibit violent behavior should be trained in acceptable techniques to restrain students.

When allegations related to corporal punishment in excess of that allowed according to board policy are brought to your attention by a staff member, a student, a parent, or the police department because of a complaint initiated by a parent, you must determine if the nature of the incident requires immediate suspension of the staff member from all duties at the school or if you should initiate the regular misconduct procedures of the school district. If the incident requires immediate suspension of the staff member, refer to Chapter 2, "Serious Misconduct Requiring Immediate Suspension." If you decide to follow the regular misconduct procedures, however, you must still conduct a fair and objective investigation to determine if there is sufficient evidence to support the allegations. The following steps should be taken:

❑ Conduct an investigation to collect information relative to the incident.
  • Use a standard form to collect statements from all witnesses and other individuals, including the parents, who have information about the alleged incident (e.g., students, staff, secretaries) (see Sample Document 1.6). Also, provide a diagram for the witness to identify body part(s) involved in the incident (see Sample Documents 1.7 and 1.8).
    — Remind the witnesses and victims to be specific and include the following:
      — when (date and time)
      — where (location or area)
      — who (first and last names of people involved or witnesses, if known)
      — what (events and actions)
    — Check the statements so that any inaccuracies, such as date or time, can be corrected by the person providing the information. If a change must be made, have the change initialed and dated by the person making the statement.

— Interview the witnesses separately and follow up with pointed questions. Probe witnesses to ensure that all information is accurate and complete.

- Take photographs of any other evidence, including the student if marks are visible on the body.
- Take photographs of the classroom or area where the incident occurred.
- Draw a diagram showing the location and any movement of persons involved.
- Check the school and district administration office files for previous progressive discipline information and/or misconduct letters.
- Collect any supplemental documentation (e.g., board policy relative to corporal punishment, staff handbook references such as Tips for Reducing Staff-Student Conflicts, School Discipline Plan, weekly bulletin references).

❑ Assess the information gathered during the investigation to determine if the misconduct section of the master contract should be invoked.

❑ Send a letter to the staff member scheduling a conference to discuss the information that has come to your attention and that might lead to allegations of misconduct (see Sample Document 1.9).

— Hold this conference as soon as possible.

❑ Prepare for the misconduct conference.

- Organize the documentation.
  — Make a copy of the students' typed statements, with the students' names omitted.
  — Make copies of all documentation for the staff member and the staff member's representative.
- Review district historical records to determine previous disciplinary action taken against other staff members accused of similar misconduct.
- Prepare an opening statement and personal notes to use as a guide during the conference.
  — Do not give the opening statement or personal notes to the staff member or the staff member's representative.

❑ Open the conference (see "The Misconduct Conference" section in Chapter 1, "General Misconduct Procedures").

- If individuals attending the conference do not know each other, introduce them.
- Cite the section of the master contract under which the conference is being conducted.
- Specify the sequence in which the testimony will be presented.
- If the staff member brings more than one person to the conference, ask the staff member to identify the person who will serve as his or her official representative. Other individuals will not be allowed to talk.

❑ Conduct the conference (see "The Misconduct Conference" section in Chapter 1, "General Misconduct Procedures").

- Present the case, including all documentation to support the allegations of misconduct.
- Permit the staff member and the staff member's representative to conduct a cross-examination and to present any pertinent documentation.
  — Be aware that the staff member's representative might try to put you on the defensive as a technique to justify the staff member's action, especially if you are perceived to have racial or gender bias.

— Do not interrupt; rather, let the staff member ramble.

— Restate and clarify the comments made by the staff member.

❑ Bring closure to the conference (see "The Misconduct Conference" section in Chapter 1, "General Misconduct Procedures").

❑ Call the staff member's representative after the conference to recommend a resolution of the misconduct charge. Possible outcomes include the following:

- If the documentation and the "preponderance of the evidence" are inadequate to support the allegation(s) that probable cause exists that misconduct occurred, inform the staff member's representative that no more action will be taken.

- If the documentation and the "preponderance of the evidence" support the allegation(s) that probable cause exists that misconduct occurred, inform the staff member's representative about the proposed disciplinary action. If the staff member's representative refuses the resolution, move to the next step of the misconduct process, which involves an impartial hearing officer (see Chapter 3, "Presenting the Misconduct Case at a Hearing"). If the staff member's representative accepts the resolution, write the letter of reprimand (see Sample Documents 10.1 and 10.2, which represent steps 2 and 3 of progressive discipline).

- If you need more time to deliberate, inform the staff member's representative that you will review the documentation and testimony before making a decision, following the contractual time line.

  — Recommend reasonable disciplinary action relative to the seriousness of the incident.

  — Be sure that consistent disciplinary action is followed for all staff members at the school or in the school district.

Sample Document 10.1
Letter of Reprimand (1)
for Using Corporal Punishment

ABC School District   Kennedy Elementary School
                                             1584 South Pineview Drive
                                             Crescent Ridge, CA 70799
                                             (916) 444-8888

January 15, 199x

Certified Mail

Mr. William Anthony
397 West Jackson Circle
Crescent Ridge, CA 70799

Dear Mr. Anthony:

This letter of reprimand is being issued for violating School Board Policy IICP, which states the following: "Corporal punishment is not an acceptable form of discipline. Physical restraint may be applied only to prevent students from harming themselves, another student, or a staff member."

During the past two months, I have discussed appropriate classroom management techniques and student discipline with you. This was necessary because I received reports from parents and students that you have been using corporal punishment in your classes.

On Tuesday, January 13, 199x, a conference was held with you in my office relative to allegations of misconduct for using corporal punishment. Mr. Darren L. Miller, ABC Educators' Association representative, was also present. At that time we discussed a situation that occurred in your classroom on Thursday, January 8, 199x. I presented statements from students and your educational assistant that substantiated the allegation that you used undue corporal punishment by holding a student's arm behind her back for about four minutes because she refused to give you a pencil. As a result, the student came to my office complaining about the pain caused by your action.

At the conference, you stated that you were upset at the time because the student did not obey your directions and that you were very sorry for your action. This is the second incident that has occurred this school year. The approved disciplinary procedures for ABC School District are outlined in the staff handbook. I remind you again that corporal punishment cannot be condoned. You must develop strategies for maintaining classroom discipline that do not include any form of corporal punishment.

This letter is a formal written reprimand and it will be placed in your personnel file at Kennedy Elementary School. You are being given an opportunity to improve your classroom management skills and comply with the policies, rules, and administrative directives of the school district. I hope you will take advantage of improving your professional performance. If you do not improve your professional conduct relative to corporal punishment, you will be subject to further disciplinary action.

If you wish to respond to this letter in writing, I must receive your response within five (5) workdays. Your statement will be attached to a copy of your letter and placed in your district personnel file.

Sincerely,

Lemmie Wade, Ph.D.
Principal

cc: Dr. Dawna M. Fitzgerald, Chief Personnel Director
    Mr. Darren L. Miller, Representative, ABC Educators' Association

Sample Document 10.2
Letter of Reprimand (2) With
Suspension for Using Corporal Punishment

ABC School District   Kennedy Elementary School
                                              1584 South Pineview Drive
                                              Crescent Ridge, CA 70799
                                              (916) 444-8888

March 26, 199x

Certified Mail

Mr. William Anthony
397 West Jackson Circle
Crescent Ridge, CA 70799

Dear Mr. Anthony:

This letter of reprimand is being issued to you for continued violation of School Board Policy IICP, which clearly forbids staff members from using corporal punishment. School Board Policy IICP states the following: "Corporal punishment is not an acceptable form of discipline. Physical restraint may be applied only to prevent students from harming themselves, another student, or a staff member." In addition, the Standards of Acceptable Conduct for All Staff Members, which was distributed at the first staff meeting in August 199x, lists expectations for staff members. These standards are clear, direct, and unambiguous. Standard 13 specifically states that staff members are expected to refrain from using corporal punishment as defined by state statutes and Board of Education policy.

On Thursday, December 21, 199x, I met with you relative to an incident in which you held a student's arm behind her back and inflicted great pain. You were issued a verbal warning. Three weeks later, I held a conference with you and Mr. Darren L. Miller, ABC Educators' Association, to discuss a second incident that occurred on Thursday, January 11, 199x. At that time, I reminded you about the Standards of Acceptable Conduct for Staff Members and stated that you are responsible for improving your conduct and developing strategies for maintaining classroom discipline without using corporal punishment. Following the conference, a letter of reprimand was issued to you for pushing a student against the wall when he came into your room to give a message to his brother.

A third incident was reported. On Monday, March 18, 199x, students in your class provided written statements alleging that you pulled a female student's hair to force her out of her seat. Your continued use of corporal punishment cannot be condoned.

This formal written reprimand is given to you to inform you that you will be suspended for five (5) school days for using corporal punishment. If you fail to correct your conduct, you will be subject to further disciplinary action up to and including termination from the ABC School District.

If you wish to respond to this letter in writing, I must receive your response within five (5) workdays. Your statement will be attached to a copy of this letter and placed in your district personnel file.

Sincerely,

Lemmie Wade, Ph.D.
Principal

cc: Dr. Dawna M. Fitzgerald, Chief Personnel Director
     Mr. Darren L. Miller, Representative, ABC Teachers' Association

11 _Insubordination_

As a school administrator, be consistent when rendering staff misconduct decisions.

As the school administrator, you have the authority to set reasonable rules for all staff members to follow so they can teach children in an orderly school. Therefore you should provide all staff members with a list of standards of acceptable conduct to follow in school. These rules cannot violate discrimination laws or interfere with First Amendment freedom of speech. If a staff member willfully disregards reasonable rules, you can charge the individual with insubordination. Most insubordination cases are initiated because a staff member refuses to obey a reasonable, direct, or implied order of the school administrator. Staff members cannot ignore reasonable directives and policies of the school administrator or school board. Insubordination is often cited as cause for dismissal, especially if the staff member was repeatedly admonished about the situation.

Insubordination charges often result from conflicts in the administrator-staff member relationship. For example, despite warnings and advice, a staff member may refuse to follow a reasonable order and instead decide to follow his or her own will. But before you issue charges of insubordination, you must have evidence that the staff member knowingly and deliberately violated the rule, order, or directive.

If one or more of the following circumstances are present, insubordination cannot be sufficiently alleged or established (American Law Reports, _ALR3d,_ 1977, p. 87):

112

1. Alleged misconduct was not proved.
2. Existence of a pertinent school rule or a superior's order was not proved.
3. Pertinent rule or order was not violated.
4. Teacher tried to comply with the rule or order, but was unsuccessful.
5. Teacher had an admirable motive for violating the rule or order.
6. No harm resulted from the violation.
7. The rule or order was unreasonable.
8. The rule or order was invalid as it was beyond the authority of its maker.
9. Enforcement of the rule or order revealed possible bias or discrimination against the teacher.
10. The enforcement of the rule or order violated the staff member's First Amendment rights.

As the school administrator, you must prove beyond a reasonable doubt that the alleged misconduct occurred and that it is in violation of board policies, administrative directives, and rules of expected conduct of all staff members. You must be certain that your order to the staff member is clear and the staff member was unsuccessful in complying with the order.

If a staff member verbally refuses to carry out an order, it is not considered misconduct until he or she fails to perform the duty (Avins, 1972, p. 25). Therefore you must remind the staff member what is expected, cite the policy or rule, and inform him or her that failure to perform the duty will result in necessary disciplinary action.

When allegations related to insubordination are brought to your attention, you must determine if the nature of the incident requires immediate suspension of the staff member from all duties at the school or if you should initiate the regular misconduct procedures of the school district. If the incident requires immediate suspension of the staff member, refer to Chapter 2, "Serious Misconduct Requiring Immediate Suspension." If you decide to follow the regular misconduct procedures, however, you must still conduct a fair and objective investigation to determine if there is sufficient evidence to support the allegations. The following steps should be taken:

❑ Conduct an investigation to collect information relative to the incident.
  • Use a standard form to collect statements from all witnesses and other individuals, including the parents, who have information about the alleged incident (e.g., students, staff, secretaries) (see Sample Document 1.6).
    — Remind the witnesses and victims to be specific and include the following:
      — when (date and time)
      — where (location or area)
      — who (first and last names of people involved or witnesses, if known)
      — what (events and actions)
    — Check the statements so that the person providing the information can correct any inaccuracies, such as date or time. If a change must be made, have the change initialed and dated by the person making the statement.
    — Interview witnesses separately and follow up with pointed questions. Probe witnesses to ensure that all information is accurate and complete.

- Take photographs of any other evidence.
- Check the school and district administration office files for previous progressive discipline information and/or misconduct letters.
- Collect any supplemental documentation (e.g., board policy relative to insubordination, staff handbook references such as duty assignments, School Discipline Plan, weekly bulletin references containing notification of due dates).

❑ Assess the information collected during the investigation to determine if the misconduct section of the master contract should be invoked.

❑ Send a letter to the staff member to schedule a conference to discuss the information that has come to your attention and that might lead to allegations of misconduct (see Sample Document 1.9).

   — Hold this conference as soon as possible.

❑ Prepare for the misconduct conference.

- Organize the documentation.
  - Make a copy of students' typed statements with the students' names omitted.
  - Make copies of all documentation for the staff member and the staff member's representative.
- Review district historical records to determine previous disciplinary action against other staff members accused of similar misconduct (see sample documents in Chapter 4, "Misconduct Charge Statements").
- Prepare an opening statement and personal notes to use as a guide during the conference.
  - Do not give the opening statement or personal notes to the staff member or to the staff member's representative.

❑ Open the conference (see "The Misconduct Conference" section in Chapter 1, "General Misconduct Procedures").

- If individuals attending the conference do not know each other, introduce them.
- Cite the section of the master contract under which the conference is being conducted.
- Specify the sequence in which the testimony will be presented.
- If the staff member brings more than one person to the conference, ask the staff member to identify the person who will serve as his or her official representative. Other individuals will not be allowed to talk.

❑ Conduct the conference (see "The Misconduct Conference" section in Chapter 1, "General Misconduct Procedures").

- Present the case, including all documentation to support the allegations of misconduct.
- Permit the staff member and the staff member's representative to conduct a cross-examination and to present any pertinent documentation.
  - Be aware that the staff member's representative might try to put you on the defensive as a technique to justify the staff member's action, especially if you are perceived to have racial or gender bias.
  - Do not interrupt; rather, let the staff member ramble.
  - Restate and clarify the comments made by the staff member.

❑ Bring closure to the conference (see "The Misconduct Conference" section in Chapter 1, "General Misconduct Procedures").

❑ After the conference, call the staff member's representative to recommend a resolution of the misconduct charge. Possible outcomes include the following:

- If the documentation and the "preponderance of the evidence" are inadequate to support the allegation(s) that probable cause exists that misconduct occurred, inform the staff member's representative that no further action will be taken (see Sample Document 2.2).

- If the documentation and the "preponderance of the evidence" support the allegation(s) that probable cause exists that misconduct occurred, inform the staff member's representative about the proposed disciplinary action. If the staff member's representative refuses the resolution, move to the next step of the misconduct process, which involves an impartial hearing officer (see Chapter 3, "Presenting the Misconduct Case at a Hearing"). If the staff member's representative accepts the resolution, write the letter of reprimand (see Sample Documents 11.1 and 11.2, which represent steps 2 and 3 of progressive discipline).

- If more time is needed to deliberate, inform the staff member's representative that you will review the documentation and testimony before making a decision, following the contractual time line.

  — Recommend reasonable disciplinary action relative to the seriousness of the incident.

  — Be sure that you follow consistent disciplinary action for all staff members at the school or in the school district.

Sample Document 11.1
Letter of Reprimand (1) for Insubordination

ABC School District   Estrada High School
                                                              1955 Orchard Road
                                                           Crescent Ridge, CA 70799
                                                               (916) 444-2222

October 3, 199x

Certified Mail

Ms. Inez Bartlain
871 Park Lane
Crescent Ridge, CA 70799

Dear Ms. Bartlain:

This letter of reprimand is being issued to you for your insubordinate conduct in refusing to follow a reasonable request from me to escort your students to the cafeteria. According to State Statutes and Board policy, I am empowered to successfully operate the school. Also, all staff members are expected to abide by the Standards of Acceptable Conduct given to them in the handbook on August 24, 199x, the first day of school.

On Tuesday, September 12, 199x, I orally reprimanded you during a conference in my office for refusing to accept an additional social studies class during the fourth hour. I told you that student enrollment had increased in September by over 60 students; therefore additional classes were added to the teaching schedule. Also, I told you that requiring you to teach that class complied with the provisions of Board policy and the master contract. You told me that you were opposed to teaching that class, but added that you would do it. I reminded you about item 2 in the Standards of Acceptable Conduct, which states that staff members are to "perform duties assigned."

During a misconduct conference that was held on Monday, October 2, 199x, I told you that, even after I gave you directions to escort your fourth hour social studies class to the cafeteria, you continued to allow your students to go to the cafeteria unsupervised. As a result, one of your students was involved in a fight near the cafeteria. In addition, other staff members reported that your students were so noisy that they could not teach. At the end of the conference, I gave you a clear and direct order to stop willfully disregarding my reasonable orders to escort your students to the cafeteria.

This letter serves as an official reprimand for your insubordinate conduct for failure to escort your students to the cafeteria. I am giving you another chance to improve, and I hope that you will take the opportunity to correct your conduct. Failure to comply with this directive will be considered as insubordination, and you will be subject to further disciplinary action.

If you wish to respond to this letter in writing, I must receive your response within five (5) workdays. Your statement will be attached to a copy of this letter and placed in your district personnel file.

Sincerely,

Benjamin Najam
Principal

cc: Dr. Dawna M. Fitzgerald, Chief Personnel Director, ABC School District
Mr. Samuel Denison, Representative, ABC Educators' Association

Sample Document 11.2
Letter of Reprimand (2) With
Suspension for Insubordination

ABC School District   Estrada High School
                                                      1599 Orchard Road
                                                 Crescent Ridge, CA 70799
                                                      (916) 444-2222

November 17, 199x

Certified Mail

Ms. Inez Bartlain
871 Park Lane
Crescent Ridge, CA 70799

Dear Ms. Bartlain:

This letter is a formal written reprimand to take disciplinary action against you for refusing to let me into your classroom to conduct an observation of your second hour social studies class on Wednesday, November 1, 199x. On the first day of school, I gave you and all staff members a copy of the Standards of Acceptable Conduct, which covers the behavior expected of staff.

I verbally reprimanded you on Tuesday, September 12, 199x, about your refusal to accept an additional social studies class. At that conference, you had an opportunity to discuss your views relative to that allegation. I reminded you that you, as well as other staff members, must follow reasonable rules. In addition, on Monday, October 2, 199x, a conference was held in my office to remind you about your responsibility to follow reasonable directives from me. Again, I orally reprimanded you about not escorting your students to the cafeteria or to the rest rooms.

On Wednesday, November 15, 199x, I held a misconduct conference with you regarding your failure to let me conduct a performance evaluation of your second hour social studies class on Wednesday, November 1, 199x. Specifically, I tried to enter your room at approximately 10:15 a.m. to observe your teaching. Because your door was locked, I used my master key to enter your room. You were sitting at your desk, and your students were talking loudly. Then, you got out of your chair and asked me not to evaluate you because you had no prior notice of my visitation. You further stated, in the presence of your students, that I could not observe your class.

I want to state as emphatically as possible that I have the right to conduct performance evaluations of all staff members at Estrada High School. My right to conduct such performance evaluations is a statutory right as well as a contractual right. Moreover, no teacher has the right to deny the principal an opportunity to conduct a performance evaluation.

This letter serves as an official reprimand for your insubordinate conduct. I am recommending that you be suspended for one (1) day without pay. Also, I want to clearly state that, if you engage in further insubordinate conduct, you will be subject to more severe disciplinary action up to and including termination from the ABC School District.

If you wish to respond to this letter in writing, I must receive your response within five (5) workdays. Your statement will be attached to a copy of this letter and placed in your district personnel file.

Sincerely,

Benjamin Najam
Principal

cc: Dr. Dawna M. Fitzgerald, Chief Personnel Director, ABC School District
    Mr. Samuel Denison, Representative, ABC Educators' Association

12 *Neglect of Duty*

As a school administrator, you must make the tough misconduct decisions and avoid telling the staff member: "I had nothing to do with it . . . he made me do it." "I had to do it. . . . I was forced to do it."

Neglect of duty arises when a staff member fails to carry out assigned duties. If the staff member's duties are well defined in written format in the staff handbook and if the staff member received a written description of the duty to be performed, neglect of duty can be proven without difficulty.

School staff members have a variety of duties to perform to ensure a safe, orderly environment for children and to keep the school operating efficiently. The duties of staff members are critical to the proper supervision of children during the time they are under the care of the school. The proper supervision of children is usually set forth in board policies, the master contract, and local school rules. No child is to be left unsupervised while he or she is under the care of school authorities. Therefore you must be emphatic and clear regarding the list of acceptable conduct of staff members, in particular, supervising students. In addition, you should provide to staff members a list of school duties and the names of staff members responsible for various assignments. Also include a description of all duty assignments in the staff handbook.

A fine line can exist between misconduct and evaluation of a staff member, especially related to neglect of duty. For example, failure to grade students' papers may be construed as misconduct but would more appropriately be presented in the evaluation of the staff member.

120

When allegations related to neglect of duty are brought to your attention, you must determine if the nature of the incident requires the staff person to be suspended immediately from all duties at the school or if you should initiate the regular misconduct procedures of the school district. If the incident requires immediate suspension of the staff member, refer to Chapter 2, "Serious Misconduct Requiring Immediate Suspension." If you decide to follow the regular misconduct procedures, however, you must still conduct a fair and objective investigation to determine if there is sufficient evidence to support the allegations. The following steps should be taken:

❑ Conduct an investigation to collect information relative to the incident.
- Use a standard form to collect statements from all witnesses and other individuals, including the parents, who have information about the alleged incident (e.g., students, staff, secretaries) (see Sample Document 1.6).
  — Remind the witnesses to be specific and include the following:
  — when (date and time)
  — where (location or area)
  — who (first and last names of people involved or witnesses, if known)
  — what (events and actions)
  — Check the statements so that any inaccuracies such as date or time can be corrected by the person providing the information. If a change must be made, have the change initiated and dated by the person making the statement.
  — Interview witnesses separately and follow up with pointed questions. Probe witnesses to ensure that all information is accurate and complete.
- Take photographs of the classroom or area where the incident occurred.
- Draw a diagram showing the location and any movement of persons involved.
- Check the school and district administration office files for previous progressive discipline information and/or misconduct letters.
- Collect any supplemental documentation (e.g., board policy, staff handbook references such as duty assignments and procedures for filing reports and taking attendance, weekly bulletin references for due dates for reports).

❑ Assess the information collected during the investigation to determine if the misconduct section of the master contract should be invoked.

❑ Send a letter to the staff member scheduling a conference to discuss the information that has come to your attention that might lead to allegations of misconduct (see Sample Document 1.9).
  — Hold this conference as soon as possible.

❑ Prepare for the misconduct conference.
- Organize the documentation.
  — Make a copy of the students' typed statements with the students' names omitted.
  — Make copies of all documentation for the staff member and the staff member's representative.
- Review district historical records to determine previous disciplinary action against other staff members accused of similar misconduct (see sample documents in Chapter 4, "Misconduct Charge Statements").

- Prepare an opening statement and personal notes to use as a guide during the conference.
    — Do not give the opening statement or personal notes to the staff member or the staff member's representative.
❏ Open the conference (see "The Misconduct Conference" section in Chapter 1, "General Misconduct Procedures").
- If individuals attending the conference do not know each other, introduce them.
- Cite the section of the master contract under which the conference is being conducted.
- Specify the sequence in which the testimony will be presented.
- If the staff member brings more than one person to the conference, ask the staff member to identify the person who will serve as his or her official representative. Other individuals will not be allowed to talk.
❏ Conduct the conference (see "The Misconduct Conference" section in Chapter 1, "General Misconduct Procedures").
- Present the case, including all documentation to support the allegations of misconduct.
- Permit the staff member and the staff member's representative to conduct a cross-examination and to present any pertinent documentation.
    — Be aware that the staff member's representative might try to put you on the defensive as a technique to justify the staff member's action, especially if you are perceived to have racial or gender bias.
    — Do not interrupt; rather, let the staff member ramble.
    — Restate and clarify the comments made by the staff member.
❏ Bring closure to the conference (see "The Misconduct Conference" section in Chapter 1, "General Misconduct Procedures").
❏ After the conference, call the staff member's representative to recommend a resolution of the misconduct charge. Possible outcomes include the following:
- If the documentation and the "preponderance of the evidence" are inadequate to support the allegation(s) that probable cause exists that misconduct occurred, inform the staff member's representative that no more action will be taken.
- If the documentation and the "preponderance of the evidence" support the allegation(s) that probable cause exists that misconduct occurred, inform the staff member's representative about the proposed disciplinary action. If the staff representative refuses the resolution, then to move the next step of the misconduct process, which involves an impartial hearing officer (see Chapter 3, "Presenting the Misconduct Case at a Hearing"). If the staff member's representative agrees with the resolution, write the letter of reprimand (see Sample Documents 12.1 and 12.2, which represent steps 2 and 3 of progressive discipline).
- If more time is needed to deliberate, inform the staff member's representative that you will review the documentation and testimony before making a decision, following the contractual time line.
    — Recommend reasonable disciplinary action relative to the seriousness of the incident.
    — Be sure that consistent disciplinary action is followed for all staff members at the school or in the school district.

Sample Document 12.1
Letter of Reprimand (1) for Neglect of Duty

ABC School District   Duffy Middle School
                                                   543 Orange Drive
                                              Crescent Ridge, CA 70799
                                                   (916) 444-3333

September 14, 199x

Certified Mail

Mr. Michael VanderMurr
482 West Valencia Court
Crescent Ridge, CA 70799

Dear Mr. VanderMurr:

This letter is a formal reprimand for failure to supervise students during the time they were under your supervision at school. Although one of your duties is to escort students to and from the cafeteria during the fourth period, you failed to carry out this assignment on both Monday, September 6, and Wednesday, September 8, 199x.

During the incident that took place on September 8, some of your students ran to the cafeteria, making excessive noise that disturbed classes on the first and second floors. Also, two female students in your class were involved in a fight near the cafeteria. Security staff and another teacher broke up that fight, but both students were suspended from school. When I questioned you about escorting students to the cafeteria, you said that you allowed your students to walk to the cafeteria without you and that this was a daily routine for them.

The proper supervision of students is covered in board policies, the master contract, and the staff handbook. Moreover, on the first day of school (Thursday, August 27, 199x), you and all staff members received a copy of the Standards of Acceptable Conduct for Staff Members. The standards are clear, direct, and unambiguous. Standard 9 specifically states that staff members are to "refrain from leaving students unsupervised." In addition, a list of the Standards of Acceptable Conduct for Staff Members is shown on page 39 of the staff handbook. The Weekly Staff Bulletin dated September 8, 199x, states the school procedure for escorting students to the cafeteria for lunch.

I suggest that you read page 21 of the staff handbook, which explains the procedures for escorting students to and from the cafeteria as well as outlining general guidelines for the proper supervision of students. You should also speak with other teachers in your unit about the correct procedure for escorting students to the cafeteria.

This letter serves as an official reprimand for failure to escort your students to the cafeteria on September 6 and September 8, 199x. You are being given another chance to comply with this reasonable request to escort your students. I hope you will take advantage of this opportunity to correct this situation and that further action will be unnecessary.

If you wish to respond to this letter in writing, I must receive your response within five (5) workdays. A copy of your statement will be attached to this letter and placed in your district personnel file.

Sincerely,

Manuel Rodriguez
Principal

cc: Dr. Dawna M. Fitzgerald, Chief Personnel Director, ABC School District
     Ms. Lucy Erickson, Representative, ABC Educators' Association

Sample Document 12.2
Letter of Reprimand (2) With
Suspension for Neglect of Duty

ABC School District

Duffy Middle School
543 Orange Drive
Crescent Ridge, CA 70799
(916) 444-3333

October 28, 199x

Certified Mail

Mr. Michael VanderMurr
482 West Valencia Court
Crescent Ridge, CA 70799

Dear Mr. VanderMurr:

This letter of reprimand is being sent to you for failure to report to after-school bus duty. On Tuesday, October 26, 199x, you were assigned to supervise the after-school bus departure area in front of the school building. Two other teachers and two teacher assistants were also assigned to supervise the bus departure area. These individuals reported to duty on that day, but you did not. As you know, duty schedules are developed on a monthly basis in collaboration with all teachers and are published in the weekly bulletin.

I gave you a letter of reprimand dated September 14, 199x, for failure to escort your students to the cafeteria. At that time, I warned you that you must comply with my reasonable order to escort your students to the cafeteria during their lunch hour, and I reminded you that all staff members must obey the Standards of Acceptable Staff Conduct. These rules are clear, direct, and unambiguous. Standard 9 says that staff members are to "refrain from leaving students unsupervised." Also, I suggested that you read pages 21 through 29 of the staff handbook, which explain the procedures on the proper supervision of students.

This letter serves as an official reprimand for neglect of duty and failure to report to after-school bus duty on October 26, 199x. Because you have failed to follow previous oral and written reprimands, I recommend that you be suspended without pay for one (1) day. I am also stating as clearly as possible that you are responsible for providing supervision for your students. If you fail to correct your conduct, you will subject yourself to further disciplinary action.

If you wish to respond to this letter in writing, I must receive your response within five (5) workdays. A copy of your statement will be attached to this letter and placed in your district personnel file.

Sincerely,

Manuel Rodriguez
Principal

cc: Dr. Dawna M. Fitzgerald, Chief Personnel Director, ABC School District
     Ms. Lucy Erickson, Representative, ABC Educators' Association

13 *Tardiness*

As a school administrator, use a mistake in handling a misconduct case as a learning experience but not as an excuse to take no formal action in the future.

State education departments require children to attend school a specified number of days per year and set the number of hours per school day. The hours per day are converted into school starting and closing times in agreement with the teachers' association, which bargains with the board of education on the teachers' hours, wages, and working conditions. Moreover, the local school administrator clarifies when staff members are to report to work and when they are to leave at the end of the school day.

School policy with regard to staff member tardiness should be clearly specified in detail and distributed to all staff members at the beginning of the school year. You must provide a list of standards of acceptable conduct for staff members, including the expectations that they be on time for work. All staff members must be warned that violation of the tardiness rule may result in disciplinary action. In the staff handbook, spell out the tardiness policy of the school and consequences for tardiness. For instance, if a staff member is tardy to work three times, a verbal reprimand is given to the staff member. Thereafter, any additional tardiness to work will result in payroll reductions and, if necessary, further disciplinary action.

As the school administrator, you must be aware of extenuating circumstances that may hinder a staff member from reporting to work on time, and you should consider the staff member's record before you take disciplinary action. If a staff member has a consistent pattern of arriving late to work or leaving early, you must take action so the staff member knows what conduct is expected of all staff members. Nevertheless, it is the staff member's responsibility to correct problems that are causing the tardiness (e.g., car that will not start, alarm clock that does not work, child care employee who is undependable). Whatever the situation, you must enforce the policies fairly and evenly for all staff members.

When allegations related to tardiness are brought to your attention, you must follow the regular misconduct procedures of the school district and conduct a fair and objective investigation to determine if there is sufficient evidence to support the allegations. The following steps should be taken:

❑ Conduct an investigation to collect information relative to the incident.
- Compile a summary of the days and number of minutes tardy as well as the reasons given by the staff member.
- Check the school and district administration office files for previous progressive discipline information and/or misconduct letters.
- Collect any supplemental documentation (e.g., board policy relative to the workday, staff handbook references such as Guidelines for Tardiness, weekly bulletin references).

❑ Assess the information collected during the investigation to determine if the misconduct section of the master contract should be invoked.

❑ Send a letter to the staff member scheduling a conference to discuss the information that has come to your attention that might lead to allegations of misconduct (see Sample Document 1.9).
— Hold this conference as soon as possible.

❑ Prepare for the misconduct conference.
- Organize the documentation.
- Make copies of all documentation for the staff member and the staff member's representative.
- Review resources available to determine the recommended disciplinary action against other staff members if the evidence supports the allegations of misconduct (see sample documents in Chapter 4, "Misconduct Charge Statements").
- Prepare an opening statement and personal notes to use as a guide during the conference.
  — Do not give the opening statement or any personal notes to the staff member or the staff member's representative.

❑ Open the conference (see "The Misconduct Conference" section in Chapter 1, "General Misconduct Procedures").
- If individuals attending the conference do not know each other, introduce them.
- Cite the section of the master contract under which the conference is being conducted.
- Specify the sequence in which the testimony will be presented.
- If the staff member brings more than one person to the conference, ask the staff member to identify the person who will serve as his or her official representative. Other individuals will not be allowed to talk.

❑ Conduct the conference (see "The Misconduct Conference" section in Chapter 1, "General Misconduct Procedures").

- Present the case, including all documentation to support the allegations of misconduct.
- Permit the staff member and the staff member's representative to conduct a cross-examination and to present any pertinent documentation.
- Invite the staff member to tell you about the issue.
- Do not interrupt; rather, let the staff member ramble.
- Restate and clarify the comments made by the staff member to ensure mutual understanding.

❑ Bring closure to the conference (see "The Misconduct Conference" section in Chapter 1, "General Misconduct Procedures").

❑ After the conference, call the staff member's representative to recommend a resolution of the misconduct charge. Possible outcomes include the following:

- If the documentation and the "preponderance of the evidence" are inadequate to support the allegation(s) that probable cause exists that misconduct occurred, inform the staff member's representative that no more action will be taken.
- If the documentation and the "preponderance of the evidence" support the allegation(s) that probable cause exists that misconduct occurred, inform the staff member's representative about the proposed disciplinary action. If the staff member's representative refuses the resolution, then move to the next step of the misconduct process, which involves an impartial hearing officer (see Chapter 3, "Presenting the Misconduct Case at a Hearing"). If the staff member's representative agrees with the resolution, write the letter of reprimand (see Sample Documents 13.1 and 13.2, which represent steps 2 and 3 of progressive discipline).
- If more time is needed to deliberate, inform the staff member's representative that you will review the documentation and testimony before making a decision, following the contractual time line.
  - —Recommend reasonable disciplinary action relative to the seriousness of the incident.
  - —Be sure that consistent disciplinary action is followed for all staff members at the school or in the school district.

Sample Document 13.1
Letter of Reprimand (1) for Tardiness

ABC School District   Kennedy Elementary School
                                             1584 South Pineview Drive
                                             Crescent Ridge, CA 70799
                                                  (916) 444-8888

September 13, 199x

Certified Mail

Mr. William Anthony
397 West Jackson Circle
Crescent Ridge, CA 70799

Dear Mr. Anthony:

This letter of reprimand is being presented to you for failure to report to work at the official starting time to perform your assigned duties. The Board of Education and the ABC Educators' Association reached an agreement on hours employees work. The hours per day are converted into staff starting and ending times for staff members. Thus the school district and the ABC Educators' Association agreed on the starting time for all employees to report to work and the time for all employees to leave at the end of the school day.

On the first day of school (Thursday, August 24, 199x), all staff members were given the Standards of Acceptable Conduct. These standards are clear, direct, and unambiguous. In fact, Standard 1 states that staff members are to "report to work on time and refrain from leaving before the established time." The Standards of Acceptable Conduct are also on page 39 of the staff handbook.

Within one week, you have been late to work three times; specifically, Wednesday, September 6, Friday, September 8, and Monday, September 11, 199x.

In an effort to correct this behavior, I met with you on Friday, September 8, 199x, regarding the first two incidents. At that time I verbally warned you about your tardiness and reminded you that it is important to report to work on time to perform your duties. You stated that you were late on those days because the train stopped traffic for over 20 minutes on South 60th Street. When you were late five minutes on Wednesday, September 11, 199x, I gave you a tardy card to complete to explain your tardiness. You stated on the card that you overslept.

This letter serves as a reprimand for being late to work. I encourage you to resolve the problems that are interfering with your ability to report to work on time and assume your duties as scheduled.

If you wish to respond to this letter in writing, I must receive your response within five (5) workdays. Your statement will be attached to a copy of this letter and placed in your school personnel file.

Sincerely,

Lemmie Wade, Ph.D.
Principal

cc: Mr. Darren L. Miller, Representative, ABC Educators' Association

Sample Document 13.2
Letter of Reprimand (2) for Tardiness

ABC School District   Kennedy Elementary School
                                          1584 South Pineview Drive
                                          Crescent Ridge, CA 70799
                                             (916) 444-8888

October 27, 199x

Certified Mail

Mr. William Anthony
397 West Jackson Circle
Crescent Ridge, CA 70799

Dear Mr. Anthony:

This letter of reprimand is being presented to you for failure to report to work at the official starting time to perform your assigned duties. The Board of Education and the ABC Educators' Association reached an agreement on hours employees work. The hours per day are converted into staff starting and ending times for staff members. Thus the school district and the ABC Educators' Association agreed on the starting time for all employees to report to work and the time for all employees to leave at the end of the school day.

On the first day of school (Thursday, August 24, 199x), all staff members were given the Standards of Acceptable Conduct. These standards are clear, direct, and unambiguous. In fact, Standard 1 states that staff members are to "report to work on time and refrain from leaving before the established time." The Standards of Acceptable Conduct are also on page 39 of the staff handbook.

Specifically, you were late to school on Wednesday, September 6, Friday, September 8, and Monday, September 11, 199x. On Friday, September 8, 199x, I met with you regarding the first two incidents. At that time, I verbally warned you about your tardiness and reminded you that it is important to report to work on time to perform your duties. You stated that you were late on those days because the train stopped traffic for over 20 minutes on South 60th Street. When you were late five minutes on Wednesday, September 6, 199x, I gave you a tardy card to complete to explain your tardiness. You stated on the card that you overslept.

You were again late to work on October 4, October 12, October 16, and October 19, 199x. The time that you were tardy on the last four dates was deducted from your pay. I warned you again about the importance of reporting to work on time to assume your duties. Also, you received a tardy card for leaving the mandatory open house ten minutes early, and a deduction was made for coming late and leaving early for open house on that day.

This letter serves as a reprimand for failure to report to work on time and ready to assume your assigned duties. Although you had an opportunity to improve your conduct and to report to work on time, you have failed to make corrections. Therefore I am recommending that you be suspended for one (1) day without pay. Also, I want to state as clearly as possible that you are to report to work on time to assume your assigned duties or you will be subject to further disciplinary action.

If you wish to respond to this letter in writing, I must receive your response within five (5) workdays. Your statement will be attached to a copy of this letter and placed in your school personnel file.

Sincerely,

Lemmie Wade, Ph.D.
Principal

cc: Mr. Darren L. Miller, Representative, ABC Educators' Association

References

American Law Reports. (1977). *ALR3d cases and annotations* (Vol. 78). Rochester, NY: Lawyers Co-Operative.

Avins, A. (1972). *Penalties for misconduct on the job.* Dobbs Ferry, NY: Oceana.

Delon, F. G. (1977). *Legal controls on teacher conduct: Teacher discipline.* Topeka, KS: National Organization on Legal Problems of Education.

Halloran, J. (1981). *Supervision: The art of management.* Englewood Cliffs, NJ: Prentice Hall.

McCarty, M. M., & Cambron-McCabe, N. H. (1987). *Public school law: Teachers' and students' rights* (2nd ed.). Newton, MA: Allyn & Bacon.

Reutter, E. E., Jr. (1985). *The law of public education* (3rd ed.). Mineola, NY: Foundation Press.

Index

NOTE: Complete forms and letters are indicated by bold page numbers.